Everything You Wish to Ask A Headhunter

"*Everything You Wish to Ask A Headhunter* is a must-read for people planning for their careers. I am impressed by the information presented, especially from the headhunter's perspective. In this book, experts in the industry provide practical insights into career planning."

– Francis Koh
Managing Director, CAPITA

"This book is a fairly comprehensive compilation of what should be considered when embarking on a new career or job, by gathering experiences from professionals (and in certain instances, not-so-professionals) that would be able to assist you in your search for a new role. This book contains a career's worth of observations and tips on how to navigate, what is for most people, a minefield that can potentially lead to some very wrong things. This candid overview should provide the inexperienced or out-of-practice job seeker with a 'leg up' in what continues to be an increasingly competitive and changing landscape, and enables them to realise some of their true worth. This is an interesting guide for recruitment professionals and job seekers alike."

– Marek Danyluk
Managing Director, Argyll Scott

"Some great tips and insights from two industry experts. A must-read for anyone considering their career options."

– Ben Batten
Country General Manager, VOLT

"Steven and Adrian prove that when it comes to searching for a job and surviving in the corporate jungle, it's neither who you know, nor what you know that counts. Ultimately, it's what you do. This makes for a great read!"

– Paul Slezak
Co-founder, RecruitLoop
Co-author of *21 Things to Do to Get a New Job NOW!*

"Adrian and Steven have put together a useful career resource for jobseekers, based on their headhunting experiences, and angled to fit Singapore's context. It is easy to read—reflecting questions and issues faced by job seekers, and highlighting the importance of building skills and a positive mindset. I'm glad that the authors have produced a handy kit to guide PMEs towards better jobs."

– Gilbert Tan
CEO, Employment and Employability Institute

Everything you wish to ask

A headhunter

STEVEN PANG & ADRIAN TAN

Candid Creation Publishing

First published December 2013

Candid Creation Publishing books are available through most major bookstores in Singapore. For bulk order of our books at special quantity discounts, please email us at enquiry@candidcreation.com.

Everything You Wish to Ask A Headhunter

Authors:	Steven Pang & Adrian Tan
Publisher:	Phoon Kok Hwa
Copyeditor:	Corrine Teng
Layout:	Stephanie Kam
Published by:	Candid Creation Publishing LLP 167 Jalan Bukit Merah, #05-12 Connection One Tower 4 Singapore 150167
Website:	www.SingaporeBookPublisher.com
Facebook:	www.facebook.com/CandidCreationPublishing
Email:	enquiry@SingaporeBookPublisher.com
ISBN:	978-981-07-7643-5

National Library Board, Singapore Cataloguing-in-Publication Data

Pang, Steven, 1967- author.
Everything you wish to ask a headhunter / Steven Pang & Adrian Tan. – Singapore : Candid Creation Publishing, 2013.

pages cm.
ISBN : 978-981-07-7643-5 (paperback)

1. Job hunting. 2. Employment interviewing. 3. Career development.
I. Tan, Adrian, 1989- author. II. Title.

HF5382.7
650.14 -- dc23 OCN862953905

Printed in Singapore

ACKNOWLEDGEMENTS

This book would not have been possible without the help of Candid Creation Publishing, for going the extra mile to provide us, first-time authors, with helpful tips and advice. Thank you for offering excellent feedback, as well as suggestions, which we subsequently adopted when putting together this book.

We would also like to extend our personal thanks to our families, friends, and colleagues for lending us their greatest support. As a result, this book could be completed smoothly and on time.

CONTENTS

FOREWORD

In my current endeavour in National Trades Union Congress (NTUC) championing for workers, especially Professionals, Managers, and Executives (PMEs), I have met and spoken to thousands of PMEs. Many of them have shared with me their challenges and these engagements provided me with deep insights on the issues that many job seekers face in trying to land their dream job and career. I have come across many PMEs who are highly talented individuals with passion, motivation, and optimism. However, many may not know how to put all that together and effectively "sell" that to potential employers.

Everything You Wish to Ask a Headhunter attempts to encapsulate and puts across the necessary job seeker survival skills in a very succinct and readable format. As experienced headhunters with a wealth of experience in dealing with placements and progression, I commend and applaud the efforts put in by Adrian and Steven in painstakingly authoring and seeing to the fruition of this book. It will serve as a reachable toolkit for job seekers, especially PMEs to navigate and maneuver in the job market. Interestingly, besides the art of landing a job, the book also touches on tips in moving up in your career and getting promoted. I am sure this book will be an enjoyable read for all including new job entrants and those with varied lengths of experience in the workforce.

Patrick Tay Teck Guan
Director, NTUC LSD
Executive Secretary, HSEU
Advisor/Senior Consultant, USE

PREFACE

You are probably reading this book because you are searching, or are thinking of searching for a new job. You are perhaps seeking the elusive dream job that promises all you covet, such as career challenges, a fair or even generous compensation—essentially the perfect company that has the right culture fit for you.

Fortunately, there is no lack of jobs. In fact, there are vacant positions in most companies, but there is however, rightly or wrongly, a perceived shortage of suitable talent or skills (both hard skills and/or soft skills).

How you can benefit from reading this book

This book will reveal tips on how you can get hired! You will learn ways to be successful in your job search by tapping into your knowledge, skills, and confidence, and effectively bringing out your best. This newfound wisdom will prove to significantly increase your chance of scoring the job you desire.

Key areas to be discussed in this book include:

- Knowing what motivates and drives you.
- Branding you—identifying who are you and what you stand for.
- Crafting your very own "elevator pitch".
- Getting out on the job search battlefield and winning.
- Preparing and presenting a winning résumé.
- Skill auditing—recognising your strengths and weaknesses.
- Acing a job interview.
- Standing out by solving your potential employer's problems.

- Leveraging on social media platforms such as LinkedIn, Twitter, Facebook, YouTube, and blogs for your job search.
- Knowing the techniques to effectively negotiate salary packages.

Once you land that dream job, you will need to track your career progress through a development path that will keep you satisfied and adequately rewarded for your career contributions.

In this book, we will also share tips on surviving the corporate jungle through ways like:

- Negotiating a salary increase without coming across as a money grabber.
- Working with toxic colleagues without going insane.
- Reporting to a new employer and getting yourself on the radar as an indispensable asset to the company.
- Chairing a meeting and keeping it effective and productive.
- Learning what makes a good people leader.
- Knowing how to win a business argument and tell someone off tactfully.
- Knowing how to fire your subordinates professionally.
- Knowing proper business lunch etiquette.

In the course of our work over the years, we have been frequently bombarded with many questions by job seekers. As such, we feel that the best way to present this book is through a question-and-answer format. In this way, you need not read this book from cover to cover but instead zoom in on the most compelling questions that you have always wanted to ask. To help you identify which of us has responded to a particular question, we have used two different icons at the start of each answer:

- Steven Pang

- Adrian Tan

Let's get rolling!

PART ONE

GETTING HIRED!

"Choose a job you love, and you will never have to work a day in your life."

–Confucius

#1 How do I know it's time to change my job?

A.T

There will always come a time when the mojo is low or things just seem to become a drag. You cannot quite pinpoint what has gone wrong, but things just feel different. The following are a few scenarios you may be experiencing:

- You have been working in the company for some time and more than know the ins and outs of its operations and procedures. You also know where all the "dead bodies are buried".
- Day after day, month after month, year after year, your job pans out to be merely a means to an end to pay for your bills.
- Your passion or "fire" for the job has diminished. When your alarm goes off in the morning, you want nothing more than to lay in your bed for another five minutes.
- You do not look forward to the start of the work day; you literally have to drag your feet to work.
- You have a tendency to be late for work, often blaming train breakdowns, dizzy spells, or peak-hour traffic jams. Once at work, you have a dull, do-not-bother-me look on your face.
- You detest the look of your employer's face and cringe every time he or she walks past your cubicle.
- You are constantly thinking of what to eat for lunch, counting down the minutes to your lunch break.
- You tend to complete tasks on hand with little or no enthusiasm.
- You resist changes that the management wants to implement, often thinking that any change is redundant. You tend to spend more time complaining about your work than thinking of ways to make it more productive.

- You try to avoid regular meetings and are frequently on medical leave.
- At work, you spend a lot of time updating your Facebook, Twitter, and Instagram accounts.
- You spend more time gossiping than discussing work matters with your colleagues. You do not look forward to company's functions or get-together sessions that promote social bonding.
- You cannot wait to leave the office when the clock strikes 6pm.

If all these sound familiar to you, you are probably getting tired or "sick" of your job. Such ill sentiments towards your job can be detrimental, or at worst, lethal to your professional career. Physiologically, you are subjecting yourself to health risks that stem from an unhappy state of mind for a prolonged period.

It is only a matter of time before your employer notices your disinterest in your work. He or she may question your level of commitment and loyalty towards the company. Your employer will also have reason to believe that your negative energy would rub off on others in the company.

Laden with such ill feelings, it is then perhaps time for you to do a reality check. Reflect on whether you still enjoy your work and whether there is still growth opportunities in your job. The least that you should be doing in your career is work towards becoming a happy employee who contributes to the advancement of the company.

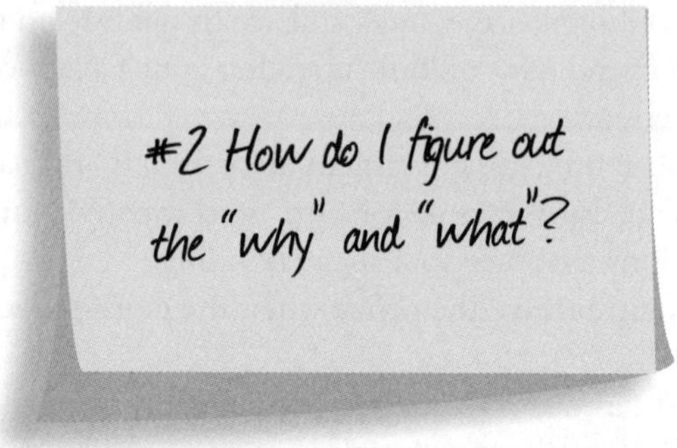

You are perhaps looking for a new career, or possibly your first job. Admittedly, this job search can prove to be an arduous task. So why not make things that much easier by first identifying the jobs that you would like to target. To get the ball rolling, make your job search process less daunting by first figuring out your "why" and "what".

Figuring out the "why"

Finding your "why" is the first step to your job search. For those who are looking for that first job, or currently unemployed, the "why" is somewhat clearer—you want to be employed.

For those who are employed, ask yourself why you are looking for a new job. What are the push factors? Are you unhappy with your superior? Do you not agree with the company's vision, values, or culture? Have you reached the glass ceiling with your employer in terms of career development and progression? Do you feel unappreciated and underpaid? Are you yearning a total shift in your career direction?

Or is it all of these reasons?

There is a saying, "Find your why before the why finds you." Do not be a victim by simply waiting for things to happen to you. Be proactive in your drive to steer your career. If things are no longer working out for you in your current job, do not wait for your employer to pull the trigger. It is better for you to resign and move on to better things, than wind up being fired and desperate for a job. So grab the bull by the horns—assess your career situation and be proactive in engineering your next move.

Another reason to be crystal clear on your "why" is so that your decision to leave would not waver should your employer counter offer. Being clear on this serves as a line in the sand to whether you should succumb to the promise of more money and an instant promotion. Why is it that the management suddenly recognises your true value when you hand in your resignation, and becomes determined to pull out all stops to retain you? Why did the management not do that before you walked in to hand your resignation letter? If the "why" stems from issues you have with your immediate superior, or because you no longer believe in the company's vision, values, or culture, then even with more money and a promotion, the fact still does not change. You will simply continue to dislike your superior and have no faith in the future of the company.

Over the years, I have seen way too many employees accept counter offers, only to leave the company six months later, because the inherent reason for leaving remains unaddressed. They have only momentarily lost focus of their "why".

So do take time to figure out your "why".

Figuring out the "what"

Assuming you are now crystal clear on your "why", the next step is figuring out "what" you want to do.

Try imaging a scenario whereby you are granted a magic wish to land your perfect career. What would this job be? What would be your job responsibilities? Would you be managing a business? Would you be leading a group of people? Would you be a sole operator and a high-level contributor? What industry would you be working in?

Figuring out the "what" requires you to perform a skill audit. You need to assess your skills and discover the type of jobs that you are motivated to do—jobs that will really get you out of bed on Monday mornings!

Do not be influenced by peer pressure when sorting these through. Just because someone you know has seemingly climbed the corporate ladder and a long impressive title to show on his or her business card, you should not feel the need to keep up with him or her if that is not your true calling.

For instance, not everyone is motivated or suited to become a people manager or business manager. Some of the most successful people I have ever had the pleasure to work with resist assuming managerial roles. They operate as lone wolves, functioning as high-level solo revenue contributors to the business and adding value that way, rather than take on the responsibility of managing people or a business.

On the flip side, also figure out what you do not want to do. Most of us learn through our past experiences. These experiences can serve as invaluable lessons in your discovery towards what it is that you want, or do not want in your next job. It is also possible that you may need to try out different things before deciding on a particular career path.

Internships, freelance jobs, and temporary jobs are all great avenues to "test drive" a career path when exploring positions or industries that you like (or dislike).

Consider current and past work experiences as well. What do you like about your current and past jobs? What have you been most successful at doing?

Another consideration when discovering your "what" is based on your moral convictions. For instance, some people will never enter the tobacco, alcohol, or the gaming industry, because it is against their moral code or religious belief.

The importance of knowing your "why" and "what"

Knowing your "why" and "what" is important—it acts like an internal compass that locks you in on a path, steering you in a direction that will lead you to your destination. It will also give you conviction and confidence in the way you portray yourself, when inevitably questioned by potential employers on your interest in a certain job. It will serve as the basis for career decisions made later in the job search process, or when you are finally offered a new job.

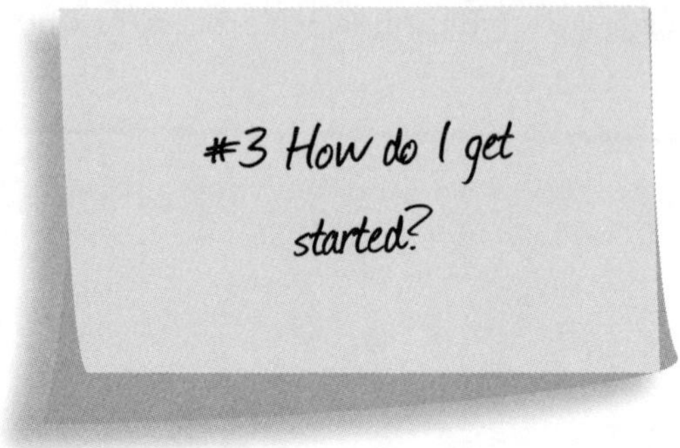

When your career compass is set and you are fully committed to a change in your career direction, the next step is to get organised.

Rightfully, your job search should become a full-time job. If you are currently unemployed, commit to spending 9am to 5pm every weekday looking for your next job. This means spending your "work hours" being on the phone calling and talking to headhunters and potential employers, sending out résumés, and responding to job openings on the various media platforms.

Once you have mentally prepared yourself for that, develop a system to keep records of potential career paths and jobs that interest you. These may be directly related to your current or past jobs, education background, or passion. Then start searching for such jobs through online searches, as well as headhunters that specialise in that field of expertise.

When it comes to job hunting, the saying, "It's not what you know, it's who you know" does hold some truth. A warm introduction or recommendation from someone who can vouch for you is always better than a cold call. List down people you know who can assist you in your job search. He or she could be someone in a position of influence or seniority—someone with business connections and networks. Once you have drawn up the list, contact these people and ask them for their support in any way possible.

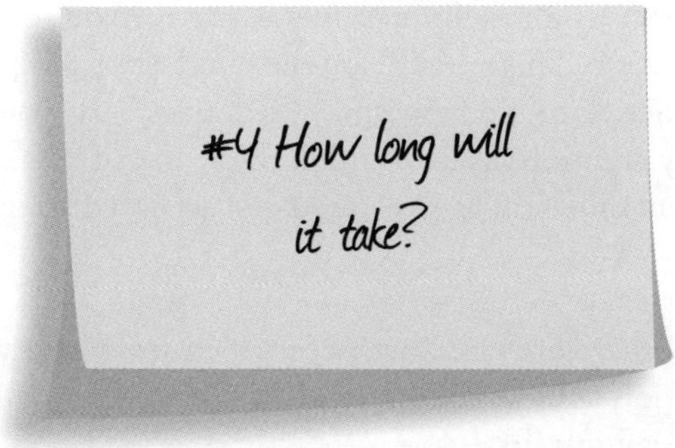

There is really no definite answer to this question as finding the right job hinges on so many factors, most of them beyond the control of the job seeker. So a better question for you to ask is: "What can I do to improve my chances of finding a job as soon as possible?"

To begin, let us first examine the external factors that will have a significant impact on your job search:

1. **Economy**
   When the economy is down, businesses tend to freeze hiring. Unemployment rate goes up and this is a time we usually refer to as the employer's market. There will be greater competition for a smaller number of job vacancies. Employers can afford to be very selective and possess a strong bargaining power when dictating a remuneration package.

2. **Type of industry**
   Sunset industries offer little or no prospects as activities on a whole are on a decline. Increasingly, labour and land intensive businesses are moving their operations to low-cost geographies.

Like in most things we do, we have a higher chance of success when we place our hearts and minds into something and give it our all. Avoid job searching only to "test the water" or check your market worth. I urge others to look into jobs only when they are serious about taking it up. Otherwise, the entire process would be a mere waste of everyone's time.

From my experience as a headhunter, it is easier for you to get a job when you are already in a job. This stems from the mindset of potential employers whose first instinct is to find possible "red flags". If you are currently unemployed, they are more likely to think the worst of you. So if possible, stay in employment until you have secured and accepted an offer with a new employer.

Having said that, there are circumstances which leave you with no choice but to leave your job anyway. Or you may have decided to take a chance by quitting your current job first.

On the average, you will need to spend approximately three months to secure a job. This includes one month to get your résumé out to potential employers or headhunters, and one month for the interview process—which in some cases, may require up to seven rounds of interviews depending on the potential employer's hiring process. The final month is then for salary negotiation, reference checking, confirmation of a commencement date, and finalising all the necessary employment contracts and paper work. Only then should you resign from your current job.

So if you are out of job and looking for a job, you will need to have a laser-like focused mind during your search. During this period, your "job" is to find a job. This means spending your typical office hours looking for your next job.

#5 Why should I understand more about myself before my job search?

As human beings, we all have a need for self-awareness whether we know it or not. From as long ago as the 1920s, with the emergence of theories from Carl Jung and research from Sigmund Freud, understanding people and their psychological types have been popularised by different people, groups, and companies.

Many tools have since been developed to encompass psychological concepts and theories, but many lack scientific backing. As such, they have been deemed largely unreliable and invalidated.

However, in more recent times, neuroscience has been adopted in our understanding of individuals and teams. Today, some of the latest assessment tools allow us to learn more about ourselves.

For instance, a system called Emergenetics® provides a framework that allows you to better understand yourself and ascertain your suitability for a type of jobs.

For many years, people have debated on the subject on whether we are completely shaped by our environment, or completely shaped by our genes. This was often referred to as the "nature versus nurture" argument. But it was probably only in the late 1990s or early 2000s that scientists came to a conclusion that nature and nurture are inseparable, each making a unique contribution to one's personality.

Emergenetics® ("Emerge" and "Genetics") is based on this theory. This theory claims that we are a result of the constantly emerging combination of genetics and environment—literally patterns of thinking and behaving that emerge from our life experiences and genetic blueprint.

Emergenetics® scientifically determined that each individual's personality can be described in terms of three Behavioural Attributes and four Thinking Attributes. Each of our attributes is shown along a spectrum. Whether you are at one end of the spectrum or the other, or in the middle for that matter, you are perfect, and unique. You are just the way you are!

One of the most exciting aspects of Emergenetics® is that it allows for infinite variations among different people—there are no types. The seven behavioural and thinking attributes can be mixed and matched at different levels to accurately describe anyone, and further, Emergenetics® is also a model that applies to both work and home.

Everyone has all the behavioural and thinking attributes, but some of these attributes come more naturally to you than the others. These attributes are called Preferences, a natural comfort level with each attribute that is reflected in his or her Emergenetics® profile. It is possible to "stretch" attributes like a rubber band when necessary, but operating outside your comfort level (in your non-preferred attributes) takes more energy and will tire you out more quickly.

Emergenetics® focuses on four Thinking Attributes—Analytical, Structural, Social, and Conceptual, and three Behavioural Attributes that affect how others perceive the Thinking Attributes—Expressiveness, Assertiveness, and Flexibility.

The Behavioural Attributes

The Behavioural Attributes are what people see first about you.

Expressiveness is your level of participation in social situations. Your degree of Expressiveness indicates how much energy you invest in connecting with others and the world around you. People who are at the quiet end of the spectrum for Expressiveness will sit sedately in a meeting, and listen more than they talk. They are considered quiet, reserved, and introspective. They prefer to avoid the spotlight, keep their feelings to themselves, and are energised by solitude.

People who are at the gregarious end of the spectrum for Expressiveness are just the opposite! You cannot possibly miss them in a meeting, since they are gregarious, talkative, and lively. They are considered outgoing, animated, and spontaneous. They prefer to seek attention, and are energised by interacting with others.

Assertiveness is your level of interest in controlling tasks and results. Your degree of Assertiveness reflects the amount of energy you invest in advancing your thoughts, feelings, and beliefs. People who are at the peacekeeping end of the spectrum for Assertiveness will prioritise harmony above having their way. They may be seen as amiable, deliberate, and diplomatic, and would prefer a gentle pace.

On the other hand, people who are at the driving end of the spectrum for Assertiveness may prioritise speaking their mind over maintaining peace and harmony. They may be considered competitive, telling, and tough, and would prefer a forceful pace.

Flexibility measures your willingness to accommodate the thoughts and actions of others. Your degree of Flexibility reflects how you prefer to respond to changes. People who are at the focused end of the spectrum for Flexibility prefer to flex within a firm and defined situation. They may be considered firm, intentional, and absolute, and prefer to stay on track. At the other end of the spectrum, people who are at the accommodating end of the spectrum for Flexibility are welcoming of changes, adaptable, and open to suggestions. They most likely would not mind interruptions, ambiguity, or change. They see all points of view, and are accepting of other people's ideas.

The Thinking Attributes

People cannot see the way you think, and what is going on in your head may be very mysterious to them.

Analytical thinking is rational, inquiring, and clear. The Analytical part of the brain wants to see data and research. People with a preference for Analytical thoughts are considered logical, cogent, and objective. They can appreciate the scientific method, and they learn by mental analysis.

Structural thinking is detailed, practical, and methodical. The Structural part of the brain follows rules and is cautious of new ideas. People with a preference for Structural thoughts are considered disciplined, organised, and conventional. They like guidelines and they learn by doing.

Social thinking is relational, collaborative, and empathic. The Social part of the brain is people-oriented and socially aware. People with a preference for Social thoughts are considered connectors and are sensitive to the feelings of others. They are intuitive about people and they learn from others.

Conceptual thinking is imaginative, unconventional, and visionary. The Conceptual part of the brain likes change and is easily bored. People with a preference for Conceptual thinking are considered inventive, original, and innovative. They are intuitive about ideas and they learn by experimenting.

By learning more about yourself through the Behavioural and Thinking Attributes introduced in Emergenetics®, you can be a better judge of job types that suit your unique personality.

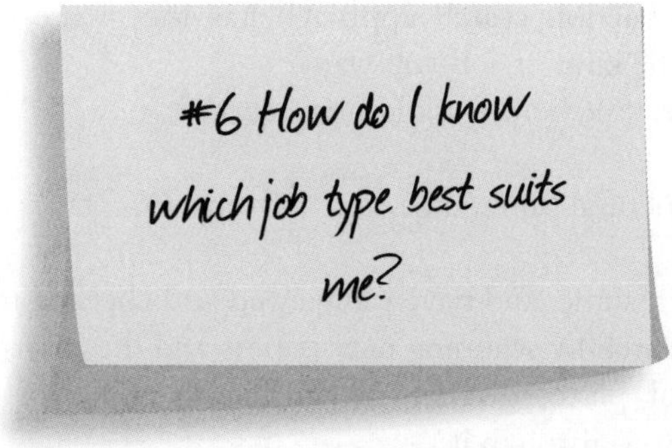

A lot of books are written about choosing the best job, and most of them, based on your temperament or skills. It is, however, very important to consider both.

If you pick a certain kind of job only because it suits your temperament, it might mean that you are not actually good at it. At the same time, there are many people who do well in jobs that they did not naturally seem inclined towards in the beginning.

So while we are unable to say that a certain type of profile—taking into consideration both thinking and behavioural preferences—is best suited for a certain job, it is important to consider both your skill sets and also what naturally keeps you motivated. Failing which, an ill-suited job will leave you tired and drained as you force yourself to operate out of our non-preferred attributes.

Applying Emergenetics®: Looking for a new job

So how can you go about getting a new job by applying Emergenetics®? The following is useful information based on your preference type.

If you have an Analytical preference, you will tend to:

- Examine your career direction and goals.
- Think about what makes you happy and consider the type of work that will bring you to that state.

- Determine what job search approach has the greatest likelihood of landing you the kind of job you want.
- Email your résumé before a job interview.

If you have a Structural preference, you will tend to:

- Update your résumé, and have it reviewed and checked for errors.
- Begin your search by scanning newspapers and the Internet.
- Make a list of places that you would like to apply for jobs with and systematically go through it.
- Prepare several copies of your résumé for an impending job interview, as well as confirm your references beforehand.

If you have a Social preference, you will tend to:

- Make contact with personal friends for job opportunities.
- Network with friends of friends to discuss possible career paths.
- Set up informational interviews with people in like industries.
- Resist the idea of preparing a formal résumé.

If you have a Conceptual preference, you will tend to:

- Ask yourself how a change of jobs would make a difference in your life ten years down the road.
- Visualise the perfect job.
- Be open to the new job when it shows up in your life.
- Create an unusual résumé, or maintain a website or blog to which you bring attention to yourself.

On the other hand, your degree of Expressiveness, Assertiveness, and Flexibility will influence how you tackle questions like "How many people will I involve in this decision?", "How quickly do I want to make a decision?", and "Have I considered all the options?", respectively.

Ideally, it is best recommended that you take into account the whole Emergenetics® approach—consider all seven attributes when searching for a new job, to ensure that you have looked into each approach. At the end of the process, it is understandable that your job search will steer towards your unique preferences.

Applying Emergenetics®: Should you accept the offer?

Supposing you are offered a new position that is very appealing. Now, you are required to make an important career decision. Here is how you might go about making it:

If you have an Analytical preference, you will tend to work out a risk/reward ratio, or list out the pros and cons before accepting a new job.

If you have a Structural preference, you will tend to make a list of practical considerations, such as travelling duration and the route taken to reach the office each day.

If you have a Social preference, you will tend to contemplate any relational consequences of a new job, and consider the thoughts and feelings of those close to you.

If you have a Conceptual preference, you will tend to meditate or reflect upon the impacts of changing your position.

Essentially, options are always available. Whatever your type, make a decision that has your best interest at heart and move forward!

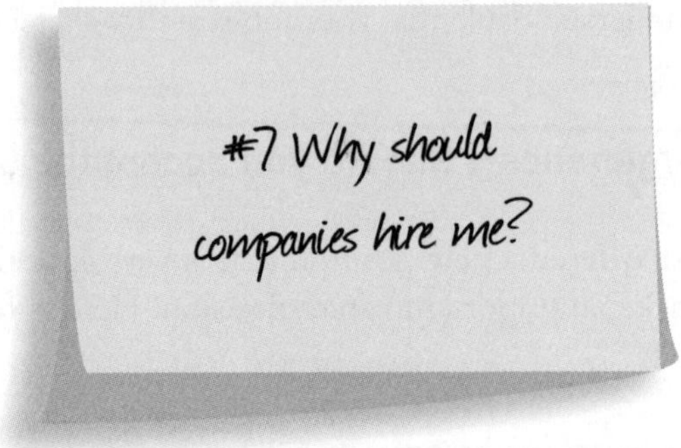

Imagine being shortlisted for a position alongside four other candidates. Supposing everyone has similar skill sets, expected salary, and education background, which candidate would the hiring manager eventually choose?

In such an instance, the deciding factor boils down to the unique selling points of each candidate—do you possess any qualities that none of the other four candidates have?

Essentially, companies are interested in you if you can make them money, or save them money. However, most candidates do not know how to put this across to potential employers.

Just think about it, a company will not be hiring if there is not already an issue or problem that needs solving. As a candidate, you must think of ways to contribute to the company. You need to help your employer make more revenue, or resolve an issue so that the company becomes more cost-efficient.

#8 Why am I still unemployed?

In the course of my work, I have come across a number of candidates who seem to be perpetually unemployed. These are candidates whom I meet at career fairs, or our job-search training workshops. Amongst them also include walk-in and write-in candidates.

I took the liberty to connect with a few of these candidates to better understand why they had been unemployed. In doing so, I was hoping to lend them a helping hand.

From what I had gathered, a small group remained unemployed as a result of a medical condition that required them to receive frequent treatments, or are suffering from complications that resulted from past injuries. These I empathise. However, the bulk of these job seekers do not carry any medical conditions. And some of these perpetual job seekers can be categorised by type:

1. **The Full-of-themselves**
   I often run into these candidates. An example of one such candidate kept interrupting my speech during a job-search workshop, citing his inventiveness on a few ideas I was sharing. It was interesting that I was just approaching a slide on "making an impression"; he sure made one, albeit a very bad one.

2. **Mr Perfect**
   I got to know this other candidate through a referral. He was a little full of himself—citing the legislation he helped create, and the minister he

queued up in the canteen with during his secondary school days. But when I looked at his résumé, I found that he had ten different roles over the past eight years. And some others were not even listed! When asked for a reason, he gave the "It's not me, it's them" explanation for turning away from jobs. Such circumstances can be analogous to dating—if all ten different girlfriends cannot stand you, the problem is least likely them!

3. **The Depressor**
   This group of candidates sigh a lot when over the phone with recruiters. They want to only engage contract or temporary jobs so that they can move on when a problem surfaces. They are candidates who aim at landing a clerical job when they are perhaps equipped with a degree in accountancy. Such candidates never fail to add gloom to anyone's day. Think about it, nobody likes to hear a sad story all day long. If you need an avenue to vent, try a helpline, not a recruiter's phone line.

4. **The IT un-savvy**
   Sometime back, I hired a temporary staff to help with very basic data entry work. Then, I had a very helpful colleague who would arrive first and help start up all the computers. On a particular morning when he was absent, I stepped into the office only to find the new temporary staff sitting at her workstation in front of a black screen. Upon questioning her, we found out that she did not know how to switch on the computer. So I can only conclude that in the age of push-mail and social media, no one can afford to be a dinosaur—not unless you are Warren Buffett!

5. **The Hot-tempered**
   I once interviewed a lady with quite a tricky track record. With her frequent change of jobs, I naturally wanted to know her reasons for leaving her past jobs. The first two, as I was told, resulted because the companies closed down. Fine, since I have never heard of those companies. But even with one of her more recent jobs at a premium club located in Singapore's prime district, she cited the closing down of the club as her reason for leaving. And just as I was about to question her about it, only because I had passed the club just days before, her face turned red as she raised her voice at me: "Excuse me! I said it closed

down!" Taken aback by her violent response, I literally jumped in my seat. At the back of my mind, I could not help but think of what she might have hurled at me if I had continued to question her!

So if I have to sum it all up, it is really all about honing good communication skills to better connect with others. Like it or not, many things you want in life do not come from isolation. You will need to speak up and ask for it. And the approach in which you ask others for help will determine the level of assistance you will be receiving, or the size of the rock that will be hurled your way. So if you keep failing in your endeavours to find a job, you probably need some communication lessons, not so much a recruiter yet.

#9 Is getting retrenched the end of my career?

AT

Getting laid off and having to search for another job can be a real bummer. Some struggle to find a new job, and with a new job, they make a lot lesser money than before.

Before I founded RecruitPlus Consulting, I was a salaried employee. And over that span of four years as a salaried employee, I was laid off not once, but twice. But like all experiences in life, there are lessons to be learnt. The following are lessons that these setbacks taught me:

1. **Setbacks can be turned into breakthroughs**
   I was offered a job after my second layoff. But the fear of being laid off for the third time plagued me. It did not help that I was offered a job in the aviation industry, which had to deal with harsh times during the SARS period. Then, people were afraid to travel and business was extremely slow. The fear of losing my job again got me thinking. I realised that the only way to prevent another layoff would be to become an employer. And so that sown the seed for the company that I now lead.

2. **Action is required for results**
   The hardest thing about losing your job is facing that large, black hole of uncertainty. It is the fear of the unknown and this fear can be paralysing. However, it is important to not let that paralysis set in. Instead, action is key. Once you toast your farewell, start dusting off your curriculum vitae (CV) and get the word out that you are looking for a job.

3. **Every industry has a life cycle**
I worked in the teaching industry when I was first laid off. Then, we provided IT-centric enrichment courses targeted at school children. Even though the money was good, our better than expected run ended when the dot-com bubble burst. Competitors started to fold and even the Ministry of Education (MOE) cut back on its budget. Naivety blinded me from the obvious that the industry was a goner. I continued to join a smaller outfit with the same business model and that was when I got laid off again.

4. **The need to know your finances**
So you are cash strapped now that you are laid off. How are you going to pay the bills? How much do you have in savings? How long can your savings last? Assessing your financial situation and gauging your ability to survive can be terrifying, but also eye opening. You might learn that you are a lot closer to the edge than you thought. Or you could find comfort in the fact that you will actually be okay, at least for a while. Either way, knowing your finances is a practical start as you plan ahead.

5. **Importance of self-reflection**
After I decided to become an entrepreneur, I then asked myself which field should I enter. As you figure out your next step, it is important to reflect on meaningful questions. When you are re-evaluating your career, you need to take a hard look at yourself. Be honest with yourself. Ask yourself what skill sets you have. Reflect upon your strengths and weaknesses. Being truly honest with yourself means throwing your ego and pride out of the window. If training is necessary, check on available courses out there. For me, I love helping my friends search for jobs. I will go to the extent of helping them answer post-interview questionnaires. So quite naturally, I got into my current field of work.

6. **Perseverance counts**
The feelings of frustration and rejection are part of any job search, but are amplified when you are already unemployed. Recognise that this can be a trying time and accept it. If you feel like you need a break and cannot possibly attend yet another interview, try doing something meaningful like volunteer work, or simply take up a new hobby. Allow

these outlets to take your mind off your job search and provide you with new perspectives on things.

Being laid off can be really daunting. But I managed to walk away from the experiences learning a lot. In retrospect, I learned to cope with rejection, deal with failure, assess my options, and more importantly, build a deeper skill set. I feel like I have weathered a storm and have come out of it a better person. The process had really been an invaluable experience as it built my resilience and character. After all, if you have never failed, you would not know what success is.

PART TWO

MARKETING YOU!

"You can't build a reputation on what you're going to do."

–Confucius

#10 How do I get on the headhunters' radar?

A.T

One of the most common questions asked by candidates headhunted is, "How did you obtain my contact?" Well, I can only say we have our ways. But surely, the candidate must have done something right to have raised his or her exposure level, even without knowing it.

Sure, they might seem to be a lucky lot. But for the rest who are still waiting for that call from headhunters, here are things that you need to do to be placed on the radar.

1. **Be prominent in online searches**
   You may have an outstanding résumé, but it must reach your target employers. It is a pity that some senior managers whom I speak with do not even know what LinkedIn is all about. What about monster.com? Do they sell monsters? Yet, these two job portals, like many other prominent job portals, are online domains where you should be featured prominently. And it does not stop with the creation of an account per se. You will need to fill it up with content, comprising of keywords that you would want to be associated with when headhunters search for potential candidates online. And always update and refine your profile—no one wants to read a profile that was last updated two years ago.

2. **Connect with peers and industry influencers who will refer you**
   Social media has made it very easy to connect with peers, colleagues, friends, and even enemies with a click of the button. In many cases, who you know is more important than the skill set you possess. And with

many companies dangling huge carrots to encourage internal referrals, a referral is really a win-win for both parties—you win a job and they win a bonus!

3. **Find the right headhunter**
   In the world of recruitment, our network is our most precious asset. No headhunter can possibly provide the same level of penetration for every network segment. So if an engineer knocks on the door of a pharmaceutical headhunter, he can break all his knuckles and still would not receive a reply. It is therefore important for you to spend some time to get to the bottom of a headhunter's specialisation and determine how that matches your job search objectives.

4. **Provide information relevant to your industry**
   Notice how some bloggers have millions of subscribers and some you just want to erase from your memory? With the wealth of information online, we are naturally drawn to certain blogs because of its value to us. They provide information that engages us and we are urged to read on. So one way of getting noticed is to start a career blog and Twitter account to jot down your nuggets of knowledge. This would help broadcast your worth, thus positioning yourself as a domain expert.

5. **Attend industry events and seminars**
   Do you follow the US presidential election campaigns? During such campaigns, both candidates are out and about speaking with people, carrying babies, and taking pictures with the general public, in the hopes of rallying support. Similarly, you need to be out there. You need to be seen and heard even if you hate it. Between an armchair general and a soldier at the war front, the latter is seen as more credible, while the former is not even seen!

#11 Why do I need an "elevator pitch"?

Supposing you have a scheduled interview with Company ABC and arrangements have been made for you to meet with the HR Director at 9am on Monday morning. You arrive at 8:55am at the Level 1 reception of Company ABC, only to find the HR Director already waiting for you.

She says apologetically: "I know I have a 9am interview with you, but my CEO has just asked me up to Level 32 for a crisis meeting. Why don't you step into the elevator with me, and in the next 30 seconds in the elevator, tell me all about you. We can decide after that whether we should reschedule for another meeting."

Now this is what is famously known as the "elevator pitch". Within 30 seconds, you have to provide a very convincing summary of yourself to warrant a second meeting.

The "elevator pitch" also comes in handy when you meet random people at parties, networking events, or conferences. When someone comes up to you and says, "Hello, what do you do?" your "elevator pitch" can be put to use. So it pays to prepare your "elevator pitch" and know it at the tip of your tongue.

The following acronym will help you prepare your 30-second "elevator pitch": S.I.R.

S = Special
What is special about what you do, or about you as a person?

I = Insights
What insights do you have? What unique value can you bring to the table?

R = Results
What have been your past successes?

When crafting your "elevator pitch", bear in mind an old Australian saying, "Sell the sizzle! Not the sausage." This means that you should not just talk about the features, but sell the benefits!

For example, having a Master of Business Administration (MBA) is a "feature". But the "benefits" of an MBA is increased exposure, as well as a deeper knowledge behind the running of all aspects of a business. Another important benefit is the opportunity to network with high-calibre individuals whom you will meet during the course.

Once you have your "elevator pitch" drafted out, practise, practise, and practise until you know it even in your sleep.

To help you get started, the following is a sample "elevator pitch" for your reference:

Hi, Mr HR Director, thank you for your time. Since I only have 30 seconds to impress you, let me get to it! My name is Paul Wong. I am a trained accountant with more than eight years of experience in handling and managing the entire spectrum of accountancy in Singapore and across Asia. My specialty lies in corporate financing, particularly for supply chain companies. I recently managed a complex project to improve productivity and maximise profits across Asia. I also helped my current company save $5 million a year via a new business model for our global multinational clients and re-financing of our long-term debts. I am about to secure my CPA and am already holding a Degree in Accountancy from University of New South Wales, Australia. Having lived in Australia and travelled across Asia for work has given me a special insight into the cultural nuances and commercial aspects of business in the Asia Pacific region.

#12 Why should I brand myself?

Why do we buy certain brands over others? Be it personal care products, sporting apparels, skin care products, cosmetics, automobiles, or luxury goods, is there a brand that we prefer over another?

According to branding experts, we choose to buy a product of a certain brand over another, because we are taken by what the brand stands for. According to these experts, we are captivated by the brand promise—encompassing its value, quality, and image.

And sure enough, as a fitness buff I only buy Adidas apparels. Why not Nike or Puma, you might ask. Well, because in my impression, Adidas epitomises high performance, durability, and a proven track record—values that I resonate with. Hence, my loyalty towards Adidas.

So let me ask you, if you are a brand, what would you be? What does your brand stand for? What are your brand values? What sets your brand apart from the others?

Thinking of yourself as a personal brand is a creative way of narrating your story in an interview. Once you have decided on your personal brand, write it down. Identify your values and worth, and incorporate your personal branding into your "elevator pitch". They will also come in handy when you are asked about your personality in interviews.

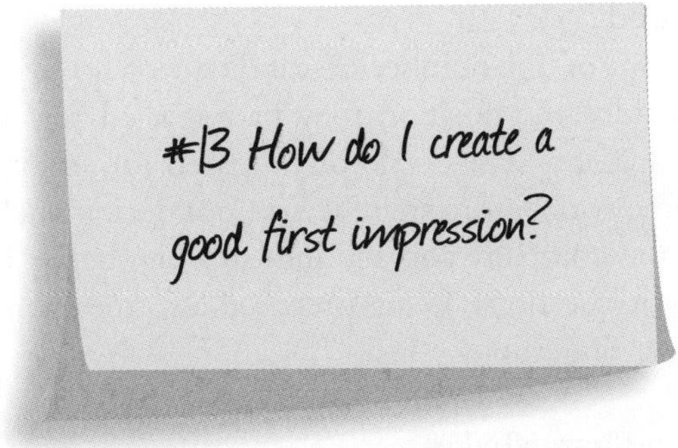

In the course of my work, I have seen and interviewed tonnes of candidates. Since our clients pay us top dollar to earmark top talent that fit their criteria 110%, not many candidates who came through our door eventually made it.

Sadly, many rejected candidates were highly educated and even well-experienced. However, they did not quite make the cut as they did not leave an impression even if their life depended on it.

So based on what I have seen and heard over the years, the following are pointers to note so that you do not sabotage your next interview. In fact, it could help create that good first impression.

1. **Dress appropriately for an interview**
   The interview is mostly over if you arrive in a pair of jeans while your interviewer is dressed in a suit. Even if you are interviewing at Google or Facebook, where formalities seem trivial, you need to dress up for the very first interview. Making an effort to dress up demonstrates professionalism and your respect for the company. If you really want to leave an impression, enquire about the interview dress code and align your attire accordingly. Needless to say, a plunging neckline is a no-no, unless my client is hiring a cleavage. Otherwise, dress appropriately so that nothing distracts the interviewer from discovering your merits career-wise.

2. Arrive prepared

I have lost count of the number of candidates who sat across me with absolutely no idea the position they had applied for. What could be worse that being at a loss? So do be prepared for an interview. Do the necessary homework before an interview, not during one! The more you know about the company and the industry, the better the chances of asking the right questions. Being prepared also means having the right answers at your fingertips.

3. Extend a good handshake

A handshake is an opener to any interview. But I am very surprised that few actually get it right. I am more surprised that many career-coaching workshops never quite discuss the importance of a good handshake. Over the years, in fact, I realised that I have only shaken fingers, fists, sweaty palms (just imagine that), and in some instances, a slapping handshake or a high-five of some sort!

But in the corporate world at least, the handshake has been a long-standing tradition since time immemorial. So if you cannot even get a 3-second handshake right, can you imagine how the next 30 minutes would pan out?

So let me get it straight—a good handshake should be firm, and accompanied with a smile and eye contact. That would demonstrate confidence oozing out from you.

4. No ring-ring and "Hello?"

If you ever watched a movie with an inconsiderate audience, you will know how frustrating it gets when a mobile phone starts ringing in the middle of something. It gets worse when they answer the call and start talking. Do they really think we cannot hear their conversation?

By far, one of my most frustrating interview encounters was a candidate who picked up a call and spoke for a good 30 seconds, while I sat re-appreciating the decoration of my meeting room. Could the phone not be set on silent mode? Is the world going to come to an end just because a call has been missed? So if anything, your lack of social etiquette speaks volume.

5. **Display a body language that shows professionalism**
   Rocking your chair, eyes panning around the room, slouching, and yawning are not exactly behaviours that read professionalism. Mind you, you will be seated in an interview chair, not the couch in your living room. As such, always maintain eye contact with your interviewer when you are speaking. Sit upright and do not slouch. Show interest in your interview. Nod your head at appropriate times to acknowledge what has been conveyed by the interviewer.

6. **Do not be all money-minded**
   Money-mindedness is more prevalent among graduate job seekers and the younger candidates. However, I cannot emphasise enough the importance of finding something you love to kickstart your career with. This is a time in your life when you have no commitments like home mortgage, kids, and cars. Once you have found the thing you love to do, the money will roll in naturally. So learn about a position first. To be paid a fair wage is to be expected, but most importantly, assess how well you can perform at the job, ascertain your level of passion, and find out if your team members are easy to work with. For sure, you will need some time to figure these out. So sleep on it and only talk about the salary once you know the job better.

7. **Display a personality**
   iPhone Siri seemingly has more personality than some of the candidates I speak with. Unless you are a robot, which would actually work out great in a factory setting, try to exhibit a personality that will cast you in a positive light. It helps to be personable. Find common grounds with your interviewer. Perhaps, she is wearing a brand that you fancy, or a pair of heels that you have been eyeing for the longest time. A common interest can help get your conversation going. For example, I once considered hiring a lady who had zero experience in the job that she was applying for, because she was also into roller-hockey. So even though it did not work out for her eventually, it does suggest the

halo effect even seasoned headhunter like me will fall into. So turn that common interest to your advantage!

8. **Follow up after an interview**
   I am not suggesting that you bug your interviewers constantly, but a simple one-off thank you note is a good gesture that helps the interviewer remember you. After all, they do interview tonnes of candidates and chances are they cannot remember every single one, not unless you remind them with a follow-up. I reckon that probably one in 30 candidates write a follow-up after an interview. So would it pay to be that one in 30?

#14 Is networking important?

Not so long ago, it is not possible to bring a camera phone to an army camp in Singapore. Going back to camp brings one back to eight years ago, when smartphones were not yet popularised. So on one occasion when I was due for my in-camp training, without my time-sapping iPhone, my camp mates and I did the next best thing—we talked.

Through our many conversations, I learned so much about all my section mates—what they did and what they had intended to buy. By taking the time to speak with one another, we bonded quite naturally. With some time to spare, we talked about everything under the sun—be it our love lives, cars, work, food, football, and even airplane crashes.

And I believe this is what networking is all about—meeting up with complete strangers and knowing them well enough to help one another out. It was during one of our gatherings when a section mate got introduced to his current job by someone he just met over a poker game.

Our in-camp stint might have given us a convenient setting to network—as we had to spend two weeks with one another—but it should not be any different in a corporate networking event.

So yes, networking can be helpful. The following are some tips that may help you when networking with others:

1. **Contribute to networking events**
   Sponsor the event and/or volunteer to help—you will gain more visibility by doing so. For instance, two street soccer sessions were organised during our in-camp stint, and for both sessions, I took the initiative to bring the ball and fix a time and date for the game to take place.

2. **Smile**
   People like to do business with others they like and feel comfortable being around. Unless you are selling your frown, let others see your smiley face.

3. **Identify common grounds to tread on**
   As a headhunter, a common ground would be discussing job opportunities, as most people are always open to a better job. If your common ground with others is not as obvious, research on individuals who will be attending these sessions, and find out more about his or her background, identify aspects of his or her life which could be relevant to yours. One avenue to learn about someone is LinkedIn.

4. **Prepare your "elevator pitch"**
   Out of point or overrun are the most common mistakes especially amongst newbies. Get to the point and use it as your litmus test to gauge interest. If they have questions, chances are they are interested.

5. **Allocate your time efficiently**
   Always move on in networking; even in speed-dating events, you get to switch prospects. A good way to move along to others is to subtly introduce another person into the conversation and slip away for a drink refill.

6. **Be approachable**
   Do not hide your phone as a way to refrain from taking down someone's contact. It is ruder than telling the guy you got the wrong target.

So I have listed some pointers to note. But do not just memorise them, it is the execution that will bear fruits. Get out there and start networking!

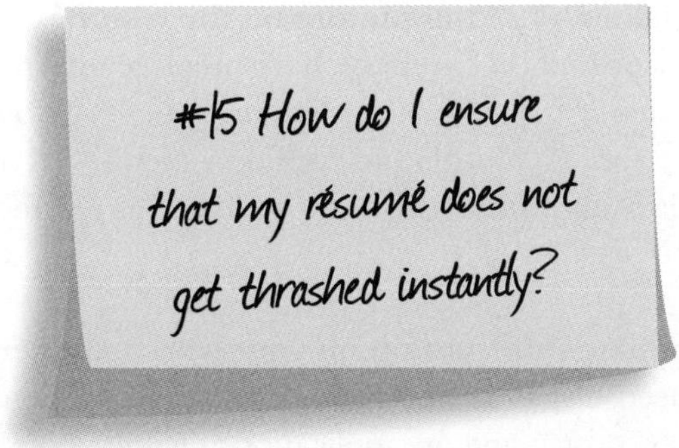

When an employer is presented with dozens of applications, he or she will try to narrow down this list quickly. By way of elimination, résumés that reflect mistakes simply would not make the cut.

Understandably, there are dos and don'ts with résumé writing. Learn to be wiser and avoid making grave mistakes, lest your résumé lands straight in the trash bin.

1. **Attach a cover letter**
   Failing to include a cover letter is an indication that you have failed to put in that extra ten minutes, which is never a good thing. And without a cover letter, you fail to personalise the message that you wish to send across, as well as set the tone of your application. Sadly, there are candidates who miss out on attaching a cover letter, and most headhunters would not hesitate to delete their applications in the first instance.

2. **Apply for the correct job**
   This happens so often—candidates get so caught up in applying for as many jobs as possible that they accidentally send their résumé and cover letter to the wrong companies. That, or they apply for an engineering position, but tell of a career objective that they really want to be a top salesperson. When a headhunter sees an application that is addressed wrongly, it will get thrashed immediately.

3. **Use a professional-looking picture on the résumé**
   Casual photos posted on Facebook have no place on a résumé. Instead, stick to the use of professional-looking photos—you are after all applying for a job. If you plan to include a picture of you posing in a tank top or drinking with friends, you are better off without a picture at all.

4. **Provide adequate information on your work experience**
   Employers need to gather as much information, in as much details as possible, when processing an application. Listing down only your job titles under "Work Experience" will not do. If you provide little or no details on your work experience, headhunters will assume just that—you have neither accounted for anything nor any great achievements to speak of.

#16 What are some résumé-writing mistakes to avoid?

A.T More often than not, a potential employer's first impression of you comes in the form of a résumé, a simple piece of paper that includes your work and educational background, typically kept within one to two pages. And this is not just in Singapore, but in the corporate scenes everywhere.

With such limited space to convey such important information, it pays to make sure you get it right the first time.

Having screened hundreds of résumés each week over the past nine years, I have identified seven of the most common mistakes candidates make when writing their résumés. While avoiding these mistakes would not automatically land you the job of your choice, it will ensure that you are at least on the right track.

1. **Unprofessional, dated, or even missing photo**
   In the age of infographics, any visual presentation that is not deemed appealing falls short. Do not be misled by supposed experts who claim that the inclusion of a photo encourages unfair employment. That may be the practice in the west, but we Asians are still a superficial bunch.

2. **Unreasonable salary expectations**
   Just because your investment banking friend got a 50% pay increment does not mean that you can go around asking for the same percentage increase. Different industries come with different parameters, and you may have forgotten that your friend's 50% increment stems from wearing three hats at work, and toiling through 16-hour work days.

3. **Lapse in work history**
   So your last job was from January 2008 to December 2009. And your current job is from January 2009 to.... wait a minute! Why is there an overlap of jobs? This, for instance, is the worst oversight you can commit in a résumé. If you can be so careless in a two-page document, would you not be making bigger, more consequential mistakes in future?

4. **Spelling or grammatical mistakes**
   Your résumé is your one chance to make an impression. A typo or misspelled word can lead an employer to believe that you would not be a meticulous, detail-oriented employee. Using a spell-check software is not enough, if a phrase like "managing steak holders" gets the green light. Instead, get a few friends to proofread your résumé. Ensure that it is free of spelling and grammatical errors.

5. **One-liner job descriptions**
   A full-time job that takes up 44 hours a week cannot possibly be condensed into a single sentence. Describing your work with just a line reflects the shallowness of your work rendered over the course of your past employment. On the other hand, depth in your work will suggest that you are a master of your trade.

6. **Inconsistent font types or poor alignment of text**
   While the most important part of your résumé is the content, there is no question that the document's overall look and feel is just as important. An illogical order, disorganised information, and inconsistent format make your résumé difficult to read. Instead, ensure consistency in the presentation of your contents—this means uniform formatting and bulleting. It will prevent potential employers from thinking that you had copied information and pasted them on your résumé.

#17 How do I create a winning résumé?

According to the study "Keeping an eye on recruiter behavior" conducted by The Ladders *(www.theladders.com)*, an average headhunter only spends six seconds looking at a résumé. Within this short time, they would have well determined whether you are a good fit for the job.

So writing a winning résumé is important. But what is the purpose of a résumé?

Most people think the résumé is a document that highlights everything about their career. But I beg to differ. In my opinion, the résumé is a selling document and the only purpose that a résumé serves is to get you that first interview. That is all a résumé is.

It is during that in-person interview phase where you begin to verbalise every single relevant detail of your career, if required.

So how many pages should a résumé span? Ideally, a résumé should span two to three pages. Anything more than that becomes too long and wordy. If you have decades of experience under your belt, just include relevant experiences from the last eight to ten years. What you did 25 years ago is no longer relevant to the job you are applying for now!

In a résumé, you should also customise, customise, customise. A winning résumé should be customised to relate to the job that you are applying for. Highlight keywords, place emphasis on core relevant skills and experiences. As much as possible, remove irrelevant content.

Now, let us look at how you can truly craft a solid résumé.

In a good résumé, the first page should include the following:

1. **An executive summary**
   This should include a few paragraphs from your "elevator pitch". Headhunters and employers tend to focus their eyeballs on the executive summary when they first look at a résumé. A good executive summary will rouse the attention and curiosity of headhunters and employers, prompting them to read the rest of the résumé.

2. **A list of your specialities**
   Your résumé will be parsed or uploaded onto a database. Listing your specialities makes it easier for the artificial intelligence on the database system to pick up on your key skills and competencies and make them searchable fields.

3. **Personal details**
   The following are must-haves:

   - **Name**
     This is pretty straightforward.

   - **Telephone number**
     Preferably a mobile number so that you can be easily reached. Avoid using an office number as this lacks confidentiality.

   - **Email**
     Preferably a personal email, as opposed to a company email. Some companies perform routine scans on their employees' emails, and through which, they might chance upon your intention to leave.

   - **Nationality**
     State your nationality and if possible, your legal status and eligibility to work in the country for the job applied. Obviously, clearance to work in the country will increase your chance of getting an interview.

- **Language skills**
  State your level of competence—be it fluent, business, or conversational. Be careful not to "talk up" your ability because you just might get tested in the interview. If you are applying for a job that requires you to have dealings in China, Mandarin would be a key language to highlight if you are well-versed in it.

- **Education**
  Most employers are a stickler on qualifications. Highlight your highest level of qualification with a "completed" side note to state that you have graduated from that course.

Information that is deemed optional in a résumé includes a personal photo of yourself, your date of birth, gender, sexual orientation, details of spouse or children, weight, height, and religion. In some countries, where the anti-discrimination laws are strict, candidates do not have to supply all these information at all.

So an example of the first page goes something like that:

Resume

A true Asia-Pacific citizen, I have enjoyed successful stints in Australia, Singapore, and Japan throughout my 17+ years working in the executive search, recruitment industry.

Over the last 17 years, I have established, developed, and led successful sales/recruitment businesses and teams across various industry verticals (technology, industrial, consumer goods, medical/healthcare) across Asia while based in Sydney, Singapore and Tokyo.

Specialities: general management, sales management, recruitment, executive search

(to be continued)

Name	John Doe
Contact details	+65 1234 5678 or johndoe99x@gmail.com
Date of Birth	X January 19XX
Citizenship	Australian Citizen & Singapore Permanent Resident
Language Skills	English (native) Mandarin (business) Japanese (conversational, lived 4.5 years in Japan)
Education	University of Sydney, Australia Bachelor of Economics 19XX

(continued)

The next couple of pages in your résumé should cover your employment history, and it should include the following:

1. **Company name and description**
   The headhunter or employer may not be aware of what your company does, especially if it is a humble start-up. So make it plain for them to grasp by providing a one-paragraph description of your company, alongside the company's website URL. This helps facilitate their need to gather more information on the company, if so desired.

2. **Title and date of tenure**
   Both are straightforward. If your title (perhaps an internal title in a big company) does not reflect the seniority of the position, I would refrain from "creating" a more senior title because you might be questioned about it at the reference-checking stage.

3. **Responsibilities**
   Highlight five or six key responsibilities with sufficient details that are relevant to the position you are applying for. However, do not go overboard and list every single responsibility on your résumé.

4. **Achievements**
   This bit of information is missing in a lot of résumés I read. To make your career seem purposeful, and result-centric, list one or two

outstanding achievements in each listed position. This is where you showcase how much you contributed to the company by citing sales or profit figures, how much you have grown the company's business when you increased staff numbers or market share, and how much you have saved for the company through increased productivity or cost-cutting measures.

The following is an example of what this should look like:

Company X

Company X (www.company-x.com) XXXX headquartered executive search and recruitment firm specialising in the XYZ fields. Company X has 30 offices across Asia, Europe, and Australia.

Director, Asia, January 20XX – September 20XX

Responsibilities

- Profit & Loss for Asia region covering Singapore, Kuala Lumpur, Hong Kong, Tokyo. Approx XX people (X frontline reports).
- Business development at regional and local level.
- Setting, driving the strategy, sales and EBIT budgets/targets.
- Recruitment of new staff (management & staff level), inducting, training, and development.
- Performance management of under-performers.
- Brand building and marketing through social media platforms and traditional media platforms.

Achievements

Launched a new brand and a new business. Company X's 1st calendar year, Asia Region had a spectacular year and delivered an operating profit of USD X00,000.

Company Y

Company Y (www.company-y.com) is a privately owned entity, XXXX headquartered executive search and staffing firm specialising in XYZ fields. Company Y has offices in Japan, Singapore, Hong Kong, China, Malaysia, India, and Korea.

Regional Director, Asia, December 20xx – December 20XX

Responsibilities

- Profit & Loss for Asia region covering Singapore, Kuala Lumpur, Beijing, Shanghai, Hong Kong, Seoul, Mumbai, Tokyo. Approx 80+ people (8 frontline reports).
- Business development.
- Setting, driving the strategy, sales and EBIT budgets/targets.
- Recruitment of new staff (management & staff level), inducting, training, and development.
- Performance management of under performers.

Achievements

Re-structured the business to prepare the foundation for explosive growth.
As a result, achieved modest EBIT growth of 28% in 2006 (compared to 2005).
2007 was the best year. EBIT achieved 250% growth compared to 2006.

Other points to note when preparing a winning résumé:

- Use strong positive words like "driving growth", "successfully turnaround", and "outstanding performance".
- Use words to highlight skills and experiences that will be easily picked up with a Boolean search.
- There is no need to include your references in your résumé. You will be asked for your references after the final interview.
- Save the document under a name that can be easily referenced. Headhunters often go through hundreds of résumés a day, so a document name "résumé.doc" can get easily lost in the mix. An example of a good document name would be "shaun pang résumé.doc".

#18 What are some job search strategies that wouldn't work?

If a job search process is essentially marketing you to potential employers, then there would be marketing ploys that work, and those that simply do not. The following are some job search strategies to absolutely avoid to ensure that you still stand a good chance:

1. **Mass-sending the same résumé to different companies**
   In the marketing world, this approach is called direct marketing. Direct marketing can be conducted offline, through leaflets received in the letterbox, or online, through newsletters or advertisements that get directed to your inbox. Now how many of these advertisements do you personally respond to? Is it then not surprising that no headhunter or employer has gotten back to you?

   Since all you need is really one job placement at the end of the day, why waste time applying for a hundred openings to secure that one job when you can apply for just five. So aim for quality, not quantity. Be targeted and specific. Each résumé sent out should be tailored to present yourself in a way that makes you relevant to the job demands.

2. **Sending the same résumé over and over again to the same company, expecting different results**
   The line between desperation and passion can be very faint. Instead of sending the same résumé umpteen times, learn to emphasise on the right thing the first time round. If you are keen on a particular company, show them why you believe you are the right person for the job. It is about tailoring your résumé to show them what they want to see.

3. **Staying at home and working the computer**

   We are so used to doing things a certain way that we become oblivious to the fact that there is more than one way to skin a cat. Instead of job searching from home, try getting yourself out among people, spreading the word about your job hunt and allowing others to see what a great employee you would make.

   Try talking to family, friends, and former colleagues. Attend business networking events and expos. Take on freelance jobs, volunteer your service, and seek consulting opportunities; they may eventually become job offers. In the meantime, keep your skills sharp and build contacts—and this is just the start!

#19 What are some effective job search channels?

A.T

Now that you have your résumé at hand, it is time to get the word out. The following are some channels you may want to consider when hunting for your next job:

1. **Monster.com**
   Monster.com is one of the largest job search engines in the world. It is also one of the main sources headhunters and employers tap into when they need to hunt for talent. This should be one of the first job boards you register with, keeping your activity level current.

2. **LinkedIn**
   LinkedIn is a social networking website for those in professional occupations. It is mainly used for professional networking. As it is free, LinkedIn has overtaken many other résumé databases to become the de facto domain for talent scouting amongst headhunters and employers. And as a job seeker, LinkedIn is simple to use and is even listed on Google.

3. **Job sites aggregator**
   Sites like Indeed.com and Recruit.net aggregate job listings from thousands of websites, including job boards, newspapers, associations, and company career pages. So as a job seeker, you just need to visit one website, instead of 10 different jobs portals. As they operate on a pay-per-click basis, such sites are cheaper alternatives compared to posting on jobs portals, and have gained significant traction with many headhunters and hiring companies.

4. **Jobs portals**

   The more prominent jobs portals in this region are JobsDB and JobStreet. They carry practically every category of job functions in all imaginable industries. If you like to be more specific, you could also head over to eFinancialCareers for positions in the finance industry, or HeadHunt Singapore for positions that pays $45,000 per annum and above. Recently, a new site RegionUp focuses on just positions that command $100,000 per annum.

5. **Newspapers and magazines**

   Albeit dwindling, a handful of companies still prefer to advertise on print publications. I would suggest just going through The Straits Time's Recruit section on Saturdays, as that usually carries the most recruitment advertisements. Industry-specific magazines are another great place to look for openings within an industry. One such example of an industry-specific magazine is Marketing Interactive for marketing-related positions.

#20 Are career fairs still relevant?

A.T

Career fairs may seem very 20th century, but they are still useful avenues. Such fairs give you exposure to the market and find out first-hand what is available.

You see, a career fair is a rather expensive setup for employers. Imagine the costs and resources involved—booking, allocating manpower, preparing collaterals and posters, on top of possibly burning a weekend. This must mean that some employers are really in need of people.

The supply of jobs is there. But surely, there is no lack of job seekers. The following are three strategies to apply so that you stand out from the crowd of job seekers:

1. **Be clear about why you are there**
   RecruitPlus Consulting does actively participate in career fairs, and to make the experience more interesting, we tend to bring along giveaways and bundle them with games so that everyone has a good time. These giveaways and games are really to entertain and ease the tension. Unfortunately, some job seekers would grumble over our giveaways, or the time it took to queue for our games—but not a single word uttered about the job opportunities available or the clients we work with. So bear in mind that a career fair is a place where you look for your next job, not a place where you pick up freebies.

2. **Wear a smile**
   A career fair could bring in hundreds of thousands of job seekers. At any one time, a recruitment firm or corporate company will only

have at most eight staff on duty. Throw in the fatigue from standing all day long, the memory is probably not as sharp. So job seekers that are usually remembered typically fall into two camps—the ones that form a really good impression and make our day, and the ones that we really want to walk away from. So stand out as the former. Put on your best smile and be that ray of sunshine.

3. **Be your own salesperson**

Most job candidates are rather one-directional. You send in your résumé and then wait for the HR to reply. In most cases, you do not hear from them at all. But the good thing about being at a career fair is that you get to interface directly with a human resource personnel and sometimes even the hiring managers. This presents the best opportunity for you to make a quick assessment of the company's requirements and ask questions.

Having said that, what you really need to do is toughen up and market yourself. Your job at the career fair is to be your own salesperson. And you cannot simply sell yourself if you do not get yourself into the thick of action and actually speak with recruiters and hiring managers.

#21 Why am I not getting a response from job boards?

A.T

Job boards (or online job boards to be exact) came about sometime in 2000. The emergence of job boards has since revolutionised the way job seekers look for a job. Gone are the days when you carry dozens of printed résumés with a minted passport photo glued on it. Or going to the post office for postage to send out that newly crafted résumé.

Instead, you now key your details on job boards once. And with a pre-created login, you can easily apply for jobs with a single click of the mouse.

Is this not fantastic? However, some factors came into play and messed up what probably could have been an excellent eco system for job searching.

You see, when every job seeker starts joining job boards and doing the very same thing, things become more complicated. Along with the ease in applying for jobs, job postings receive so much more hits. Not forgetting the influx of foreign applicants online, numbers escalate and competition grows manifold.

This alone completely overwhelms employers, as their recruit advertisements either get dropped to the bottom of the pile very quickly, or become susceptible to unwanted traffic, which is really a waste of everyone's time.

If you do not already know, job boards do not really care what jobs are available. To them, traffic volume is the key performance indicator; a high traffic places them in the number one spot, and they become identified as the leading jobs portal. You see, Portal A is the leading jobs portal because there are 50,000 job postings, versus Portal B that only has 40,000 job postings.

As a result of not having found the right candidate, companies continue to post more of the same recruit advertisements. By hitting on random jobs, you help bring recruit advertisements to top spots. And with that maximum visibility, the same recruit advertisement will attract a lot more candidates.

Knowing such frustrations, job boards came up with a filter for recruitment advertisers. This filter automatically shoves your application into the garbage bin if you do not meet any of the pre-set criteria, leaving you with no chance to convince the reviewer because he or she would not even have come across your application in the first place.

I know candidates who have sent out more than 200 résumés, and yet not receive a single response. But it is no surprise if you know how job boards work for the employer and headhunter.

So on one hand, a single-click application was created for job seekers to mass apply, on the other hand, there is a filter to prevent your application from showing up at all.

If you think about the whole system, job boards work pretty much like Groupon. Everyone loves the ease of buying and the entitled savings, but there comes a time when you wonder if all these fluffs are really needed.

Knowing the pitfalls of job boards, it is crucial for you to adopt a strategy in which online job searches accounts for nothing more than 10% of all your job search channels. The remaining should comprise of a mix of networking, working with the right recruitment agencies or headhunters, strengthening your personal brand through channels like LinkedIn or blogging, and just speaking with the right people.

To put simply, a job search is not that different from an insurance agent peddling the policies he or she sells. Assuming your products are not that different from the products other insurance agents sell, your success then depends on how well you can sell yours.

#22 How can I leverage social media in my job search?

A.T In today's social media age, you simply cannot stay away from social media tools, yet stay connected to the people and things around you. Whenever I need to research on someone, I always look him or her up on LinkedIn first.

LinkedIn is set up to be the social media platform for professional networking. Occasionally, I will go on to check their Facebook and Twitter accounts, to better judge their personality and lifestyle through their posts.

When it comes to job hunting through social media means, the keyword is visibility—you need to be visible to be found. If you cannot be found, then you really do not count.

Imagine your LinkedIn profile being a website. There are hundreds of millions of websites online. When you go on Google to search for say a hotel in Bali, you will get many pages of matches. But most will only browse through the first two pages, rarely venturing beyond that.

Similarly, with over 300 million profiles on LinkedIn, you need to appear on the first two pages of a LinkedIn search. Failing which, you will not be noted by a potential headhunter or employer.

But how can you optimise your LinkedIn profile? How can you be featured when a headhunter or potential employer does a keyword-specific search?

The following are some highlighted areas for you to look into as you attempt to boost your profile:

1. **Country of residence**
   Most headhunters and employers prefer to hire locally, so make sure you state your country of residence clearly.

2. **Industry**
   Selecting the right industry sector makes you more easily found.

3. **Keywords**
   The use of keywords is critical. In order for you to show up on the first few pages of a LinkedIn search, you have to repeat keywords that define you, for example "project manager", or "oil and gas". Use these keywords as often as possible on your LinkedIn page, under sections like the "Executive Summary", "Experiences", as well as "Skills and Expertise".

4. **Number of connections**
   The more connections the merrier—preferably over 500.

5. **Experience**
   Give a good account of your work experiences. If possible, simply cut and paste information from your résumé. But be aware that since your LinkedIn profile is made totally accessible to the public, you need to practise caution when revealing information that may be sensitive. This could be your company's confidential information, such as revenue, sales, or profit figures.

6. **Skills and expertise**
   List as many of your skills and expertise as possible, especially key ones that you want to be identified with. These can be keywords like, "project manager", "project management", or "oil and gas".

7. **Groups and associations**
   Join and contribute to as many relevant industry groups and associations as possible. This will raise your visibility and grow your target audience.

8. **Education**

For some positions, having the right qualification is required. Ensure that you list out all relevant qualifications to increase your chance of getting a related job.

#23 Can my smartphone help in my job search?

A.T It is obvious that Singaporeans spend a lot of time on mobile phones. Coupled with the introduction of the tablet (I know of a three-year-old who has one and you probably do too), a computer is no longer the only electronic device from which we gather information.

However, many job seekers are still stuck in the computer era. These unassuming souls apparently process their cover letters, résumé, and even job applications in the same manner our parents did. But technological advancements have made it imperative for job seekers to move away from the "age of dinosaurs" and to start leveraging on the mobility of smartphones in order to gain that all important competitive edge.

The following are ten smartphone applications that will give you that "edge":

1. **LinkedIn by LinkedIn Corporation (Free)**
   Locally, LinkedIn has captured more than one million users and counting, and headhunters have already taken a serious adoption of LinkedIn as another useful tool to find candidates. As such, it is paramount for any serious job seeker to have a LinkedIn profile and to use it regularly to expand and extend their professional network. A wider network means increased visibility, and that will be helpful in getting the job seeker a higher chance of being headhunted.

2. **Interview Skills by Barclays Capital (Free)**
   The job interview is that first make-or-break moment in advancing your career. And it can be a genuinely nerve-wrecking experience for

most. If only you could "role-reverse" and understand exactly what the interviewer is looking for. This is what the application does. You will be given inside information on questions typically asked by employers. You will hear from three fictional candidates and get to make a hiring decision of your own. And you will then be able to compare notes with a real Barclays Capital headhunter. All in all, I reckon this application to be pretty good stuff!

3. **How to Get a Job Interview by Docstoc Inc. (Free)**
   Does job hunting leave you exhausted? Are you nervous about nailing a job interview? This application provides a complete blueprint for landing your dream job, from finding to securing it. Let professionals and job interviewers explain how to find a position that is aligned with your skills and that compensates you well. The application includes tips from actual CEOs and hiring managers on topics like:

   - Most common interview questions and the answers they are looking for.
   - How to negotiate the highest salary possible.
   - Things to avoid saying during your job interview.
   - A paragraph to include in your cover letter that will generate a response 98% of the time.
   - The top five factors that managers use to determine whether or not you get hired.

4. **JobStreet by JobStreet (Free)**
   This JobStreet application allows you to source for jobs on JobStreet.com anytime, anywhere. Once you make it through the one-time pain of signing up for an account via your desktop on JobStreet.com, you can start applying for jobs with a single click. What is worthy to note about this application is the smart use of location. If you are looking for a job in a specific area, the "Jobs Near Me" feature would display a map and what is available nearby.

5. **Résumé App by Vurgood Applications (US$2.99)**
   Within seconds of keying in your information, Résumé App will generate a professional-looking PDF résumé that is completely

customisable with whatever information you choose to include. You can input as many past job experiences as required, as well as specific education information and activities. You can input specific skill sets that you have obtained, and even extra-curricular activities if you so choose. If you desire, the application allows multiple references, as well as photographs, all of which can be included in the PDF résumé. There is also an option, to include a generic cover letter, if the destination company requires one.

6. **Job Lander by SparkRiver (Free)**
   Do you want your résumé to stand out from all the others and immediately grab the attention of headhunters and employers? Job Lander is an incredibly easy-to-use application that creates gorgeous, colourful, personalised infographics for your résumé within minutes. The colourful infographic showcases your employment and academic history with an eye-catching graphical timeline. Job Lander will make your résumé stand out and get you noticed. And that is critical when the job market is such that so many people are sending in their résumés for the same job.

7. **Facebook by Facebook Inc (Free)**
   Last but definitely not least, Facebook is not just a tool designed to idle your time away while you wait for your job applications to be processed. It is also an avenue for job seekers to engage quality companies. This will keep you in the loop on new updates, trends, and even new openings, as more and more companies are putting in extraordinary resources to leverage on the power of social media. You can even join the pages of reputable recruitment agencies that frequently put up latest information immensely useful to job seekers in their attempt to find their next dream job.

So there you have it—the top mobile applications for today's job seekers!

PART THREE

SELLING YOU!

"You miss 100% of the shots you don't take."

–Wayne Gretzky

#24 How many employers should I be selling myself to?

One of the things headhunters despise most is calling up a candidate who has no recollection of the position he or she has applied for. It makes you wonder if the candidate has sent out so many résumés that he or she simply cannot remember at all. It also makes you wonder what the candidate wants. Is it in administration, or customer service, since the candidate has apparently applied in both areas?

When you decide who to sell to, you need to also analyse your success rate.

"I sent out 200 résumés but I didn't get a single interview?"

"This is my thirtieth job interview but I still didn't get a single offer?"

Such feedback is real and seems to infer that the economy is in a recession. But if it had not been so, then what had gone wrong?

Upon closer analysis, I learnt that the 200 résumés were sent out to almost every single job function. But would a company really want a jack-of-all-trade who really does not know what he or she wants?

An honest reflection on what did not go right in your previous job search will help you understand how you can fine-tune your next job search. But it will be a long and draggy nightmare if subjectivity and emotion come into play.

So ask around the people in your life. Friends and families are usually the best critics. Share your job search experiences with them, go through role plays, and try identifying areas for improvement.

Focus on your key strengths and only apply for positions that you fulfill at least 70% of the criteria. It is more effective and a lot less painful than sending out countless résumés.

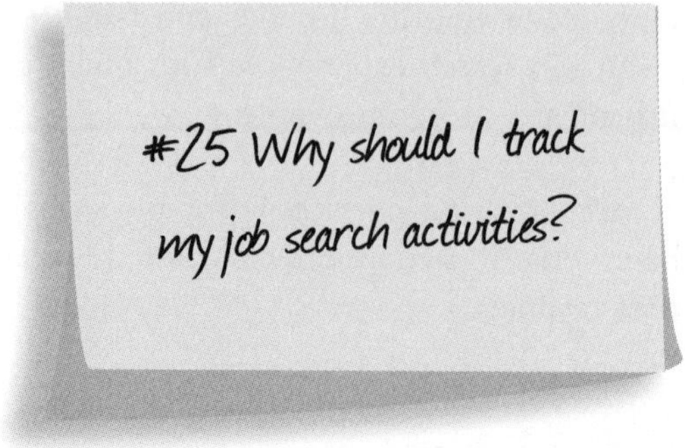

With any job application, you are essentially running a sales campaign. The objective is to sell a single product, yourself, to a pool of selected prospective customers. And with all sales positions, you need to have a target, a key performance indicator (KPI). Your KPI will serve as a barometer to help you monitor and understand how well you have been doing. After all, you cannot possibly improve what you do not measure.

Remember the guy who sent out 200 résumés, but without a single reply? Well, the one thing he did right is actually tracking his job search activities. But that is something most do not bother to do—they simply go through the motion, basing their actions on gut feelings. This would be akin to a sales person who does his job without measuring his performance whatsoever! And since your job search is effectively a sales process to sell you, measuring your activities is of paramount importance.

With this knowledge, you have to start keeping track of what you do. More importantly, you need to set KPIs on a regular basis to keep you aligned—allowing you to know if you are way ahead or fallen short of your target. That piece of information will help you fine-tune your direction along the way.

Some areas that you might want to start measuring include:

- The number of new connections, or new people you connect with. And I am not just referring to HR personnel. Any connection counts as it is always easier to enter something via the backdoor.

- The number of companies contacted and the number of résumés sent out.
- The job description of jobs applied for.
- The number of first interviews.

#26 What should I prepare before an interview?

Let us review the job search process so far.

So you have mastered your personal brand and "elevator pitch", and reciting them has become second nature. You have also prepared a winning résumé which you can customise based on the positions you are applying for, and you have been invited for an interview! Now this is show time!

The interview is a time when you impress others and leave the audience, or interviewers, wanting to know more about you.

To "wow" your audience, research on the company and the person you are meeting. For this, the Internet offers a wealth of information that might come in handy.

If this is a company that you know very little of, even after researching online, do not panic. You are probably not alone. Very often, I find corporate websites full of big generic words and jargons that do not offer much background about what a company really does. So my secret to understanding a company and what they do in layman terms is to visit www.hoovers.com, a business information website for easy-to-read information on companies. Without having to pay a cent, you can have access to a one-paragraph summary of your target company's business.

This website also provides a list of three of the company's closest competitors. With all the information, you are now able to provide an informed opinion on the company and its competitive landscape during the interview.

Another good source of accurate and easy-to-understand information is Wikipedia, the free online encyclopaedia.

Since most progressive companies have a social media presence, you have other means of researching a company—through the company's LinkedIn page, Facebook account, YouTube channel, or company blog.

With no lack of information online, there should be no excuse for you to attend an interview unprepared.

#27 How should I handle typical interview questions?

The better prepared you are, the more confident you feel, and the higher the chance of you performing your best at the interview.

The following are examples of some standard interview questions and suggestions on how to best tackle them to put you in a positive light.

Why are you interested in this job? Why are you leaving? What are the push/pull factors?

By now, you ought to have figured out your "why". You are crystal clear on your motivations and capable of articulating it well. Doing this well demonstrates decisiveness. It shows that you have a clear focus and direction.

When asked for your push factors, you should state your reasons (if any) matter-of-factly. Whatever the reason, state it once and move on. Do not harp on what is negative about your superior or your company. Do not become too emotional—you do not want to be seen as a negative, vindictive person.

If you are asked for your pull factors for wanting a particular job, be truthful and show your enthusiasm, without appearing overly desperate to join the company.

What is your ideal job? What is your next move?

Revisit your answers to "figuring your what". Be specific on what you want and what you do not want, and then make careful considerations from there.

What are your strengths? What do you do well in? What comes naturally to you?

Highlight two to three of your strong points that are relevant to the job you are applying for. Here, the key is relevancy. Do not be afraid to make bold claims of your strengths and achievements, so long as they are true. In the words of Muhammad Ali, "It ain't bragging if you can back it up!"

But if you are not aware of what your strengths are, I would suggest that you approach some close friends, colleagues, and family members—people you trust and would provide an honest assessment of your strengths. You can also review your past performances for hints of what you do best.

What are your weaknesses? What are some areas for improvement?

This is a tricky one. If you are brutally honest about your weaknesses, you may not be placing yourself in the best position. So instead, you may want to preface the answer by first saying that no one is perfect. Then proceed by discussing a weakness, only to follow it with a solution or act of how you overcame it. This way, you are really turning a weakness into a strength, by highlighting your ability to overcome challenges.

For example, one could say: "I used to be terribly disorganised. I would keep a mental note of things to do, but as you can imagine a lot of things fell through the cracks. My ex-manager, someone with obsessive complusive disorder, and a stickler for details, suggested that I write up a to-do list every day. The list keeps me organised and focused on the things I want to achieve each day, prioritising events or things of greater urgency and importance."

That sounds like a reasonable answer to the question. But one of the funniest replies I heard is, "My weakness is kryptonite."

#28 What are some unexpected interview questions?

SP

If you prepare for the unexpected, then nothing the interviewer throws at you will make you at a loss for words. Unexpected questions are, as you can imagine, questions that you least expect in an interview. The following are examples of such questions:

- If you were a brand, what would be your brand and why?
- If you were a car, what car would you be and why? And what colour would you be?
- Why is a manhole round and not square?
- How many tennis balls could you fit into a bus?
- You're going to be working 110 hours a week here. Can you even handle that?
- Why don't you have any offers yet? What's wrong with you?
- What single word would you use to describe yourself so I don't walk out of here and forget you?
- Which line on your résumé is a lie?
- If you were shrunk to the size of a pencil and put in a blender, how would you get out?
- If I told you that the only way you were going to get this job is if you let me sleep with your girlfriend, would you accept it?
- What was the toughest decision you made?

As you know, these questions have no right or wrong answers. They are designed to test your thought process, logic, reasoning ability, as well as how you react under pressure, because the pressure can be intense in some jobs, and you are required to be quick thinking.

These questions may be a test of your reasoning ability and wits, but the best way to stand out in an interview is to be the solution provider to the employer's business issues, and that requires more than wits.

So when I do recruit for retail companies, I tend to ask my candidates to visit my client's retail store to look into its visual merchandising, check out the traffic in the store, and figure out ways for improvement. So when these candidates are interviewed, they can bring up some of these observations for discussion. Imagine how impressed the interviewers would be if you have solutions to their problems without being asked!

#29 How do I deal with discrimination?

During our training workshops for job seekers, there is always concern about discrimination in a few common areas. And one of the top concerns would always be age.

Many are concerned that a potential employer would overlook their application should they reveal their age. Henceforth, some would remove all numbers that could be suggestive of their age.

But such woes are usually unfounded. My reply to them is that age should not be a handicap. Instead, it should be viewed as an asset, a testament to the vast amount of experience you have amassed. It is an indication of the mistakes made and the lessons learnt as a result—lessons that will ensure you do not make the same mistakes in your new job. Think about it, who would want to work in a company that just hires young kids who are barely out of puberty.

But of course, getting job seekers to accept this argument is not easy. Most of them just want to get employed and would jump at any job opportunity. Few would feel that they can be a valuable asset to employers. This is more so when the market is slow and every door knock counts.

To clearly understand why older folks are sometimes discriminated, we have to understand why age might be a concern from an employer's perspective. Many employers we speak with cite inability to learn new things as a key concern, especially in an age when we are so reliant on computers and technology.

So knowing this, it is clear that age itself is not the crux of discrimination. It is really the perception that an older individual would have a steeper learning curve.

So what can one do about it?

Well, one sure way is to show that an old dog can still learn new tricks, and even become really good at it. This means life-long learning and constantly updating yourself with the latest developments in the market.

Imagine a 70 years old who is not only active on Facebook, but also tweets regularly. Imagine this same person blogging about his or her life experiences periodically. Now this is someone whom I would definitely view in a different light!

Essentially, you need to show proof that you are always learning, and not just superficially. You must also be able to keep up with times; I know people with more than twenty different certifications, but these amount to nothing if they do not even know how to operate a smartphone!

#30 What are some interview scenarios that I should be prepared for?

A.T

There are different types of interview settings. Try to gather as much information as possible to help you prepare yourself for the type of interview, as well as the people interviewing you. Note that it is rare to have only one round of interview prior to a job offer. Most employers will request for several rounds of interviews to ensure that a candidate is the right skill and culture fit.

1. **One-on-one interview**
   - Most interviews are face-to-face. The most traditional is a one-on-one interview.
   - "Break the ice" early. I usually start with a conversation about the weather, the weekend that had just passed, or pass a compliment on the office or my interviewer. Essentially, it is good to get the conversation going on a good start.
   - Once the questioning starts, your focus should be drawn towards addressing what the interviewer wants to know about you. Maintain eye contact, listen, and take your time to respond.
   - Personal chemistry is important. The ability to create rapport is a "win" for you.

2. **Panel/Committee interview**
   - In this situation, there is more than one interviewer. Typically, two to ten members of a panel may conduct this part of the selection process. This is your chance to put your group management and group presentation skills on display.

- As quickly as possible, try to "read" the various personality types of interviewers and get adjusted to their roles. Find a way to connect with each interviewer.
- Remember to take your time when responding to questions. Always maintain primary eye contact with the panel member who just asked the question, but also seek eye contact with other members of the panel as you speak. A common mistake is to respond to and only make eye contact with the most senior member in the room, even though the question came from another panel member.

3. **Behavioural interview**
    - The basic premise behind this interview type is that your past behaviour is the best predictor of your future actions. Questions may be asked in any interview format—telephone, panel, or one-on-one.
    - If the employer asks behaviour-oriented questions, he or she is no longer asking hypothetical questions, but questions that must be answered based on facts.
    - Here, the interviewer is looking for results, not just activities conducted. They are listening out for names, dates, places, outcomes, and how you had contributed to a certain outcome.
    - Generally, such questions start out with "Give me an example when..." or "Tell me about a time when…"

4. **Case study interview**
    - In some interviews, you may be asked to demonstrate your problem-solving skills. The interviewer will outline a situation or provide you with a case study, and require you to formulate a plan that deals with the problem.
    - You do not have to come up with the ultimate solution. The interviewers are looking at how you apply your knowledge and skills to a real-life situation. Speak and reason aloud so interviewers have a full understanding of your thought process.
    - Before answering a case study interview question, be prepared to ask the employer questions in order to clarify and gather more information so that you can better address the question posed.

- Show that you are capable of analysing and dissecting the case study. This will likely impress your interviewer.
- It is acceptable, even encouraged, for you to bring a notepad and pen. Most interviewers will allow you to take notes and jot down thoughts as you work through the case.

5. **Telephone/Skype interview**
   - Many companies conduct telephone or Skype interviews to narrow down on a pool of candidates. Telephone or Skype interviews may also be used as a preliminary interview for candidates who do not live within reasonable travelling distance from the interviewer's office.
   - It is important to treat this interview as you would a face-to-face interview. Arrange for a conducive space and convenient time to schedule the conversation. Clear a work surface to minimise distractions.
   - Focus on the conversation. Listen to the questions carefully before answering. Since your voice is key, convey energy with inflection in your voice.
   - Have a copy of your résumé nearby as a reference.
   - Avoid using a phone with call waiting. You do not want to be interrupted during an interview.
   - Try to use a landline phone or mobile phone that does not give problems. Skype is sometimes susceptible to poor connections due to the low-quality Internet connection on the other end. So always have a Plan B ready, such as a telephone number to call, should the quality of the call be compromised.

6. **Group assessment interview**
   - A group assessment interview is usually designed to uncover the leadership potential of prospective employees who will be dealing with customers.
   - Front-runner candidates are gathered in an informal, discussion-type interview. A subject is introduced and the interviewer will start off the discussion.

- The goal of the group interview is to see how well you interact with others and how you use your knowledge and reasoning to influence others.

7. **Lunch/Dinner interview**
   - The same rules apply at a meal as in an office setting. A lunch or dinner interview may be more casual, but remember that this is a business meal and you are being watched.
   - If you arrive first, display graciousness by allowing the interviewer the better seat, perhaps one with a view.
   - Use the interview to develop common ground with your interviewer. Follow his or her lead in both the selection of food and etiquette.
   - Avoid food that requires you to use your hands and avoid ordering an alcoholic beverage even if you are encouraged by the interviewer to do so. This could be a trap if you cannot hold your drink. Under the influence of alcohol, you might reveal things that really should be kept secret.

8. **Stress interview**
   - Such interviews are more common amongst candidates applying for sales positions, and are mostly unheard of today. However, you should be aware of the signals. These interviews are usually deliberate attempts to see how you react under pressure.
   - The interviewer may be sarcastic or curt, or may keep you waiting. Do not take it personally.
   - Answer each question calmly. Ask for clarification if necessary, and never rush yourself to provide an answer.
   - The interviewer may also lapse into silence at some point during the questioning. This may be an attempt to unnerve you. Sit silently until the interviewer resumes with the questioning. If a minute goes by without a word exchanged, ask if he or she needs clarification on your last comment.

PART FOUR

CLOSING THE DEAL!

"Whenever you are asked if you can do a job, tell 'em, 'Certainly I can!' Then get busy and find out how to do it."

–Theodore Roosevelt

#31 What questions should I ask at the end of an interview?

As the war for talent continues to heat up, many companies are becoming more creative in their approach to fill up job positions. Now, it is no longer just about the job. It has evolved to become everything else. Today, things have escalated to an employee courtship. Creating employer branding, making candidates feel special, allocating expensive floor space for swanky chill-out areas in the office are just the tips of the iceberg. But as a job seeker, you need to peel away from the layer of marketing barrier to get to the core of the position.

Ultimately, it is the job that matters, not the packaging. So the following are five questions to ask your prospective employer before considering taking that leap of faith:

1. **How would you describe a typical day of work in this position?**
   A job description is adequate in depicting the requirements of the position. However, such descriptions do not provide an insight into the actual weightage of each responsibility, and how frequently it must be carried out. Having a first-hand insight will provide a clearer picture of what to expect when you take over the job.

2. **Who are my colleagues and what are they like?**
   Placing many people and personalities in the same room is bound to create conflicts. But by first knowing the people that you will be working with, you can better prepare yourself to face them eight hours a day.

3. **What do you like about this company? What has been keeping you here?**
   Everyone works for money, but then there are things that come along with the money that make one choose their current job over another. Knowing what it is will allow you to learn about the company's actual belief system. And you just need to pitch them against yours to see if the company is truly a good match for you.

4. **What are the main challenges associated to this position?**
   In any role, there are those who make it, and there are those who do not. Needless to say, you want to become the former. Having an idea of the potential challenges ahead allow you to better assess your ability to tackle them.

5. **What are some attributes of a successful employee? (Specifically to line managers)**
   As the saying goes, "One does not quit their job, they quit their boss." Your boss, or superior will be the key decision maker in your performance appraisal. Knowing his or her expectations allows you to better work your way around managing your superior.

#32 What questions should I avoid asking at the end of an interview?

A.T

The interview went really well. The interviewer likes you a lot and you feel good about the interview. All is going great… until that off-the-cuff question that came out from you.

You see, an interview is like a game of chess. Every single move is crucial and a wrong one could end the game prematurely. Knowing what is off limits is critical in your interview. So the following are some questions that you may want to hold back until prompted:

1. **How much will I be making?**
   If you are engaging a headhunter, chances are you would be told what to expect, based on industry benchmarks and the budget of the interviewing company. The interviewer may also ask for your expected salary range. However, you should never ask him or her how much you would be earning, especially during the first interview.

   So yes, double standards can be expected. But asking this makes you look like you care more about the money than the job at hand. Instead, always put across that you work for passion, instead of the sole purpose of topping up your empty bank account.

2. **Do I have to work overtime on weekends or holidays?**
   Again, there is a better way of asking the time demand of any job. Instead of risking sounding curt or even self-centred, you should instead ask what a typical day or work week is like at the office for someone in this position. This will help you learn what has been done in the past and the time commitment required in future.

3. **How quickly can I get promoted?**
Remember you are there to interview for a job to assume now, not five years later! So do not make it sound like you are only using this job as a stepping stone to your next one. Focusing on how passionate you are about this job, its projects, and realising the company's goals is a better tactic.

Having said that, there are ways to learn about job advancement opportunities. For instance, you can learn about the longevity of the average employee in the company. Find out when they joined and how long it took for them to reach where they are now. Finding out if the company has a structured training programme offers hints on how much the company emphasises on grooming its people.

4. **When is the baby due?**
Keep all personal questions out of the equation and do not refer to the interviewer casually, unless specifically instructed to do so. Build rapport in other ways by asking them about their management style or their involvement with the position being interviewed for. Company culture is another safe bet. However, do not broach the topic of drinks after work just yet, unless they do. And even so, keep your enthusiasm for alcohol in check.

#33 When do I follow up with the interviewer?

Understand the timeline at the end of interview. After emphasising how keen you are on the job opportunity, ask the interviewer, "What are the next steps from here?"

Always follow up with an email or a handwritten note a day after the interview. It is a professional gesture that will make you stand out from the rest of the candidates who did not follow up with a note.

So what happens when you do not hear from the potential employer? I would suggest that you follow up one or two weeks after the interview. Perhaps the key decision makers are travelling. However, be careful not to come across as a needy stalker. After several follow-ups, move on and concentrate on other opportunities, if you are still not receiving a definite answer.

It is good professional etiquette to copy everyone involved in the interview in your emails. This includes line managers, human resource managers, as well as headhunters that made the introduction.

#34 How can I best manage a job offer?

Congratulations! You have been informed of an offer of employment, either verbally, or via an email or document. But even at this point, note that nothing is official until you have received the contract of employment.

Once you have the contract at hand, you should read through the document thoroughly, understand all key clauses pertaining to your salary, annual leave allowances, non-compete, intellectual property ownership, and probation period, amongst others. Then comes the time when you have to negotiate your salary.

Remember to be truthful when asked about your last salary, as you might be asked to produce income tax statements for checks. Should you inflate your salary, you might risk being caught.

Do be detailed on your salary package—citing base salary paid over a period of 12 or 13 months, bonus schemes, stock options, as well as other allowances.

State exactly what it is that you want. As a headhunter, I always get my talent to tell me what they want; I will try my best to meet their expectations, but there are no guarantees. In any case, I need to be in the know.

When asked for your expected salary, it is just as important for you to know your market rate. If you are in a good enough bargaining position, then be frank about what you want. If you are not in a favourable bargaining position, but would really want the job, you might want to be more passive by saying something like: "I will leave you to make me an offer and I will consider it."

If you are asking for a significant increment from your current salary (anything more than a 20% increment), be prepared to justify why you warrant that increase.

Apart from expected salary, it is just as important to negotiate other allowances, such as sign-on bonuses, entertainment, relocation, telephone, and transport allowances, as well as extra health insurance coverages and other non-cash benefits (e.g. extra leave, sabbaticals).

Once the employer agrees to what you want, stand by your word. Do not be greedy and ask for more—do not keep changing the goal posts. Show your integrity and accept the offer based on what has been agreed.

#35 Why was I rejected when everything seemed to go well?

You just had one of the best interviews in your life. The job scope is something you had dreamed about and the people seemed extremely nice. Salary sounds fantastic too. But just one thing—you never hear from them again. So what went wrong?

The following are five reasons why a headhunter might give you a miss after what seemed to be a promising interview:

1. **Not following instructions**
   With headhunters at least, a major turn-off would be candidates who do not fill in their job application forms. Yes, I know it is indeed troublesome to fill in an application form every time you go for an interview, but unless the previous company is willing to pass on that form, there is no other way for other companies to capture that information. And by seriously filling in the form, you are telling others that you are an enthusiastic job seeker. So do fill in every field, however painstakingly, and do not simply cross out five pages of the form and write in bold "REFER TO MY RÉSUMÉ".

2. **Displaying zero enthusiasm**
   If you are contacted about a position and you sound about as thrilled as you would be if you learned about another train breakdown, you will dash your chances of getting the job. Being too laid-back can be confused for being uninterested. So if you are interested in the job, act like it. Show some enthusiasm. Show that you have a heartbeat.

Headhunters want to hire those who are excited about their work, so that the client feels upbeat too!

3. **Beating about the bush**
   Conversely, if you are not excited about a job that the headhunter has set you up with, be upfront about it. Do not fake enthusiasm only to turn down the position when you are given it. If you waste the headhunter's time, he or she will no longer want to waste any more time on you when the next opportunity comes along.

4. **Performing poorly**
   Given the increasing number of temporary and contract assignments these days, many headhunters do multiple placements for candidates. This suggests that your entire career could be placed by a single headhunter. So if you make a bad impression at a company which the headhunter had previously placed you—calling in sick on Mondays and leaving early on Fridays—you can forget about ever getting another opportunity from that headhunter.

5. **Disrespecting the headhunter**
   Some job seekers do not treat headhunters with the same respect they would give a potential employer. They show up for interviews looking like they just fell off their beds and do not take things seriously. But that obviously is a big mistake. If you do not treat the headhunter with the same consideration and respect as you would a hiring manager, you might get passed over for the position. Bear in mind that if you work with a good headhunter who likes you and is on your side, you have a better chance of getting the job you desire.

PART FIVE

SAYING GOODBYES!

"When one door closes, another opens; but we often look so long and so regretfully upon the closed door that we do not see the one which has opened for us."

–Alexander Graham Bell

#36 How should I deal with counter offers?

You have decided to take up that new job offer. The next step is handing in your resignation to your current employer.

To some, this can be a very stressful thing to do. If you are an important staff to your current employer (and we all would like to think that), be prepared for one of the following reactions:

- Your employer congratulates you on your new job offer and gives you a pat on the back as he or she shows you the door (so maybe you are not that important after all).
- Your employer begs you to stay with those misty, puppy eyes.
- Your employer emotionally blackmails you. You are told that your resignation letter is not accepted. You are even questioned about your loyalty towards the company, after so much has been "invested" in you. You are made to feel like you are indebted to your current company and employer.
- Your employer comes back with a counter offer. You are offered more money, a senior title, and you are told things that had once frustrated you would be put right.

So you leave the office feeling insulted, flattered, confused, emotional, angry, or maybe a mix of everything. It would seem very tempting to stay—better the devil you know and they did promise to make all those changes. But really, should you stay or should you go?

Before you accept that counter offer, consider the following:

- By resigning, you make it known to your employer that you have been looking for other job opportunities, and are probably unhappy. So your loyalty to the company is now in question. When promotion/raise opportunities come about, your employer will remember those who are committed and those who are not. And when the company has to make headcount cuts, the ones that are deemed less loyal will normally be the first to leave.
- Accepting a counter offer might just be an insult to your intelligence and a blow to your personal pride. Do they think you could simply be "bought" with a sudden increase in salary and a better job title? Why had they not offered you all these things in recognition of your contribution to the company earlier?
- Could the counter offer be your next raise made in advance, or simply buying time so that the company can start searching for someone to replace you?
- Statistics show that if you accept a counter offer, the probability of you voluntarily leaving in six months or being let go within a year is extremely high.
- Once the word gets out that you are receiving a higher pay and enjoying a better position because you had attempted to resign, the relationship you once enjoyed with colleagues would be filled with resentment. You may have gained some, but you lose that peer group acceptance.
- What type of company gives you what you are worthy of only when you are about to resign? And if your primary reason for leaving had been an untenable relationship with your superior or colleagues, or a misalignment with the company's values and vision, would a bigger paycheck and a flashier title change all that?

Whether you should be accepting a counter offer requires you to be decisive. It is a career decision that you alone will have to make at the end of the day. Weigh your pros and cons, strip yourself of emotions in the decision-making process and stay firm. You will be respected for it.

#37 How do I resign gracefully?

At some point in your career, you may experience a burnout, an exhaustion of some sort that pushes you to resign from your job. But before making the major decision of "firing" your employer, ask yourself if you still possess a flicker of passion and enthusiasm for your job.

Does your job irk you to the extent that you wish every single day is a public holiday? Is there anything that you or your employer can do to reignite your fire?

If upon consideration, your decision is to break away, the following are some points worth observing in order to leave your job peacefully and amicably.

1. **Notify your employer**

   Inform your employer of your decision to leave and provide your reason(s) for doing so. Remain calm and composed at all times during that discussion. Do not get into any argument or bad-mouth your company even if you are extremely unhappy about things. Your paths may cross one day.

   Assure your superior that you will attempt to complete any outstanding projects on hand before handing over your portfolio to the person taking over your responsibilities. It is never a good idea to ask for an early release if the projects you are handling are on very tight deadlines. A good handover will only show your level of commitment and dedication on a professional level.

2. **Ensure a good handover**
   Once you have decided to move on, prepare a detailed and easy-to-understand handover list for the person taking over your job. Run through your responsibilities and all outstanding tasks with your colleague to make the transition a smooth and hassle-free one. This will save you the trouble of being constantly "disturbed" by the company after starting on a new job. Inform your clients, vendors, and business associates of your last day with the company and introduce a colleague whom they can liaise with upon your departure.

3. **Be impartial**
   Avoid influencing your colleagues to resign by passing critical and biased views about the company. Your employer might come to know the truth one day and that would not reflect well on your integrity and personality. You should be responsible for your own actions. It is only right to act impartially even when you have decided to leave.

4. **Stay professional**
   Do not start coming late for work and taking frequent breaks during your notice period. You do not wish to be seen as a bad influence to colleagues slogging hard at work. Even when you have grave grievances against your company, do not even think of sabotaging your company's operational infrastructure unless you wish to have a brush with the law.

#38 How do I end with class?

In today's corporate world, it is rare for someone to spend his or her entire career with just one employer. In Singapore, two to four years between jobs has become the acceptable norm. So surely, there will come a time when you will leave your company for greener pastures.

I have a tip for you if your current employer had been good to you over the years, invested in training you, paid you promptly, and looked after your welfare—never burn bridges. It would save you from potential heartaches by not coming across as a bridge-bombing terrorist. Instead, thank the people who have been in any way responsible for your success. Thank those who have given you opportunities, nurtured, and mentored you. This is called gratitude—a worthwhile value to cultivate. So when it is time to leave, do it with class and gratitude. It just showcases your impeccable character.

Lastly, tie up all the loose ends. Do not inconvenience anyone in the process, leave no ticking time bombs behind, and no skeletons in the closet. Thank everyone for contributing to your career, and then make a clean break. Now this is class!

PART SIX

SURVIVING YOUR NEW JOB!

"There may be luck in getting a job, but there's no luck in keeping it."

–J. Ogden Armour

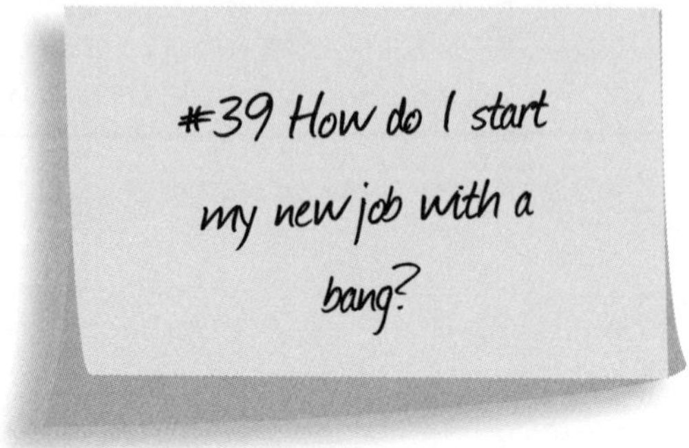

The best way to start off with your new employer is to make your entry felt with a resounding bang!

To facilitate a smooth on-boarding process with your new employer, while serving out your notice period, you could get in contact with him or her to see if any additional information is required from you as you prepare to go on board.

For a start, the new employer probably needs your mobile number for your new business cards. Decisions need to be made between choosing a laptop or desktop, between using Mac or Windows. If possible, meet for coffee with your new employer to understand how you should prepare for your new job. Show your enthusiasm and get off to a strong, positive start.

Starting your new job with a bang means making the best positive impression from day one. Be punctual, present your best, and be prepared to put your best foot forward. Should you be unable to commence work on the day that was agreed, be professional and call in to apologise, not email or text.

The following are more tips to bear in mind to ensure a smooth sailing start:

1. **Have an open mind**
   If you are a new hire in the company, adopt an open mind and embrace the new environment and people. Join your colleagues for lunch on the first day to build rapport and get to know others better. This allows you to chat with colleagues in a casual environment.

Since a new role represents new challenges, do take every new task and responsibility as an opportunity to value-add your professional life. Share past work experiences with your new colleagues, but never boast about your achievements. The last thing you want is being an outcast at work.

2. **Improve work quality**

   If you are already a senior staff in the company, chances are you are too familiar with all the work processes. As such, you might find your work somewhat monotonous—sort of like going through the motions of mundane tasks like brushing your teeth in the morning, or travelling to work in that peak-hour crowded train—things that you need to do, but with little or no enthusiasm or passion.

   To lift this monotony, try injecting some variations to your every day tasks to make it more worthwhile and enjoyable. As the saying goes, "Don't do different things. Do things differently."

3. **Avoid office politics**

   In any office setting, be it big or small, there is bound to be a certain degree of gossiping and the typical who-dislikes-who scenarios. Even though it is important to gel and get along with your colleagues, do steer clear of the "cross-firing" that goes on between fellow colleagues. Try to remain as neutral as possible. This will save you the unnecessary "flaming" and meaningless bickerings.

4. **Be approachable and upbeat**

   Be the one to offer help when another colleague is in need. Chances are you will be reciprocated in time. Share the occasional good-natured jokes with colleagues and help create a light-hearted working environment. After all, no one likes to be in a severe environment where it can be both tense and nerve-wracking. Do not overdo it though, unless you want to be regarded as the office joker or clown.

#40 What are some office personality types to steer away from?

While it is good to build rapport with colleagues, it is wise to identify those who are easy to get along with, and those whom you should avoid stepping on their toes. It pays to identify tell-tale signs of different personality types. And the following are the five most poisonous personality types—types that you should at least keep an emotional distance from.

1. **The Indian Chief**
   This person is also probably the one who brings the most fun to the office. He or she is the ringleader who suggests the extended smoke breaks, the 2-hour lunches, as well as the ganging up against a newbie because she happens to use the same lipstick colour. But the trouble comes when these bad habits rub off on you. So enjoy his or her company, but be wary of the leaving-early-coming-late attitude.

2. **The Whiner**
   They are colleagues who live on negative energy. They drag their feet to work and make damn sure that everyone in the room hears it. They may be the most hazardous to your career and your mental health. Such colleagues will take you down a path of negativity and the next thing you know, you would rather take rat poison than go to work. Your career could start to spiral downhill should your employer learn of your close association with them and the constant ranting. So it is better to have a lost friendship than a lost job, if I might add.

3. **The Princess**
   They are colleagues who always need to be rescued. They call in sick on the day of a big meeting without so much as sending you an email heads-up. You wonder how they even lived that long given their inability to even perform a simple task like filing. They drain your time and leave you feeling bitter and taken advantage of. These are partnerships that you should avoid at all costs. If necessary, enforce strict daily deadlines on such colleagues so that you never find yourself left in the lurch. Better to be the productivity police than be Simon Cowell-ed, because you are caught unprepared at the biggest meeting of your career.

4. **The Narcissist**
   They can be equally draining of your time. Their morning routine consists of going around boasting about the 99 roses they received from their boyfriends. Or how they think every guy who walks past them is a secret admirer. Enjoy their over-the-top stories and know that they are probably not going to ask how you are doing in return. Just do not give them the chance to steal your credits in the office.

5. **The Wheelbarrow**
   As the name suggests, you always have to be behind such colleagues, to lift them up, and push them along every step of the way. Once there is no more pressure, or when the watchful eyes are directed away from them, they are as useful as paint getting dried on the wall. A lot of effort is needed to get them working and they are only as good as your last push with them.

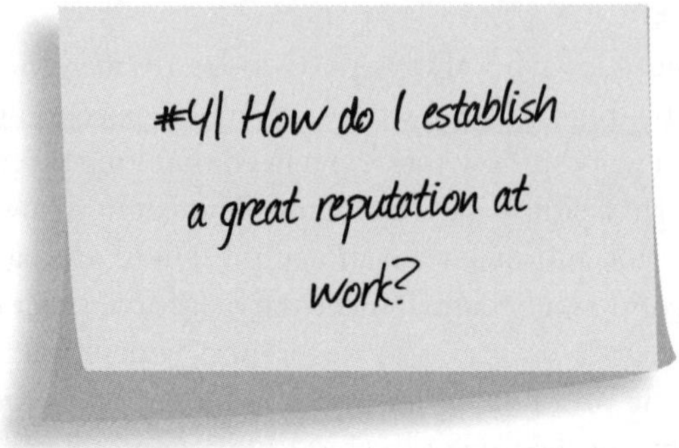

I am an unabashed fan of Mr Lee Kuan Yew, who helped transformed a tiny island with no natural resources and a huge malaria problem to become one of the major economic players and top 10 cities in the world today.

The story on the rise of Singapore has been described as one of the best the world has ever seen, even more spectacular than Athens and Rome, in their heydays. Mr Lee, in my opinion, is a "do-er".

One of the best things about Singapore's system is that success is based on meritocracy and one's intellectual aptitude, and not based on one's racial background. In fact, Singapore is as close to a true multi-cultural and multi-religious society based on cities I have seen in my many travels. It does not tolerate overt nepotism or blatant corruption, like some Asian countries. Sure, Singapore is not perfect—there are isolated cases of frustrations and trade-offs in terms of censorship and freedom of speech—but if one would look at the bigger picture, no one, not even Singapore's harshest critics, can deny that it has proven to be a very successful model.

With meritocracy, competition is intense from the time you enter the school system, right up to the time you retire at the age of 63 years old. We are told from a very young age that good work ethics and hard work will get us to the top, or at least to a respectable level in society.

This is probably why we see many "do-ers" working their butts off and delivering solid, spectacular results in the local corporate scene, and yet something seems to be missing. I have learned over time that some of these "do-ers" are terrible at promoting themselves and their achievements.

So my message for "do-ers" is to take the time to count your wins, to know what your value is, and to recognise your unique selling points. Know your "elevator pitch" and your track record of delivering successes. Once you have taken stock of your wins and successes, be ready to articulate them. Be the champion in promoting yourself through as many platforms as available. Build your self-confidence—it will come in handy when you have your performance review with your employer, when you negotiate your next pay raise, and when you have to deal with the inevitable nasty game of office politics. Most importantly, it will get you noticed and help raise your profile.

So stand up, turn up the volume, and be proud of your achievements! If you do not take credit for your hard work and contribution, someone else would—I can guarantee it!

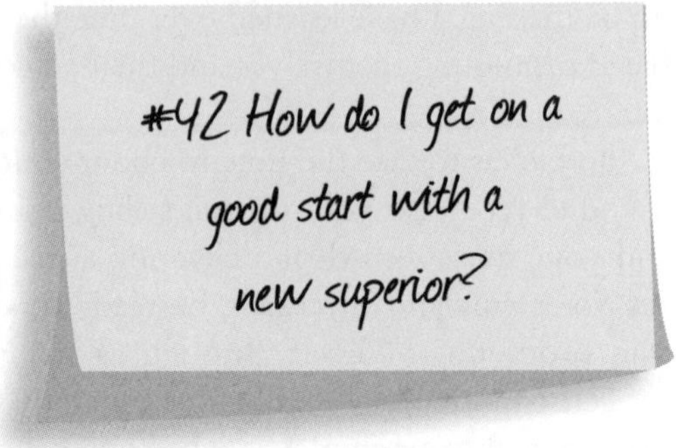

The kitchenette and water cooler huddles are buzzing with activity. A new superior has been appointed to your team. But what is the new superior like? Will things remain status quo? Will the team culture change? Will there be people who will come and go? What should I do to accommodate this change?

Getting down on the "dos"

Indeed, having a new superior on board can be rather unnerving. The following are some "dos" to kickstart this new relationship on a very positive note:

1. **Research on your new superior**
   Who is this new superior? What is he or she like? What is his or her management style or reputation? To get to the bottom of these questions, Google your superior, and look him or her under Facebook or LinkedIn. You may also want to source for information under your new superior's previous employer. Look out for media releases, business articles, professional bios, and recommendations. With people and things being so interconnected these days, the notion of six degrees of separation is not just a new-age myth. Through friends, colleagues, and other people in your network, it should not be too impossible a feat to track down those who know your new superior—people whom you can collect some anecdotal information from.

2. **Send a care package**
   When I was appointed a new position, one of my direct reports sent me a care package to help ease my transition into the new office and team. So what was in that care package? Updates on the business performance, unwritten rules, important schedules, processes, and events, cultural taboos, as well as a brief on members of the team. With a care package like that, your new superior will be very thankful. At least I was!

3. **Create an opportunity to break the ice**
   Organise a team lunch or dinner (hopefully your superior picks up the bill). The sooner everyone gets comfortable and familiar with the new superior, the sooner can the team focus on the business challenges at hand.

4. **Plan for one-on-one meetings with your new superior**
   Propose having regular one-on-one meetings, be they daily or weekly, to communicate expectations for key result areas, key performance indicators, and working style. Do not assume that the new superior has the same expectations and operates the same way your previous superior did.

   For example, he or she may want to take in information in a different format, preferring information to be delivered in a personal conversation over coffee, in a spreadsheet with numbers, or through a detailed, well-written report.

   If he or she is open to receiving constructive feedback, try sharing the following: three things he or she should continue doing, start doing, and stop doing.

5. **Give your new superior a chance**
   Your new superior will necessarily have new ideas, initiatives, and strategies—try to keep an open mind to them. Give him or her the benefit of the doubt, until proven otherwise. It may revolutionise the current mindset and ways of doing things and lift performance to a new level.

6. **Make your new superior look good**
   You can help improve the performance of the business by helping to create an open, honest, transparent, positive environment based on mutual trust. It is really win-win for all. As the saying goes, "When the tide rises, everything rises with it."

Steering away from the "don'ts"

Along with the "dos", there is a set of "don'ts" to consider as well. The following are a few examples:

1. **Don't spread rumours of your new superior**
   Word will eventually get to your new superior that you have been telling tales about him or her. Now this is certainly not a good way to build a mutually trusting relationship at work.

2. **Don't be a brown noser**
   You may come across to your new superior as someone who is insincere and too eager to please. It may also generate ill feelings among colleagues.

3. **Don't compare**
   Nobody likes to be compared. Telling your new superior "I like how the previous superior used to…" does not achieve anything. Instead, try saying, "How would you like this to be done?" Ultimately, acknowledge that a new Sheriff is in town.

4. **Don't be uncooperative**
   Do not secretly, or not so secretly for that matter hope that your new superior fails. This will only generate negative vibes and bring the morale of the team down; everyone loses in this case. Instead, give your new superior 100 days to prove his or her worth. If despite your best efforts in being the team player and doing everything right, things are still not working out, then its perhaps time to get off that train and look for a new job!

#43 What are some tips for a successful sales career?

I love what I do!

For those unfamiliar with the headhunting business and the supposed secrecy behind it—things really boil down to sales. Since day one, I have only had thoughts about meeting my sales targets in my head. As I moved up the management ladder, it shifted from individual sales targets to team sales targets, to eventually revenue and profit targets for a business that spans across Asia.

Like in any sales job, my performance and remuneration are closely tied to my ability, as well as my troop's ability to deliver the numbers.

Unlike in a typical sales job, I do not sell widgets or a definite product and service. Instead, I sell a premium professional service to my clients (or employers) and my pool of talent. It is a high-touch business, having to work with people, provide business solutions, solve business issues, and work with talent on their career goals and aspirations.

As a salesman of some sort, I am naturally a positive thinking, can-do, optimist—well I have to be! I am a practical optimist, I might say. In the earlier years of my career, I naively thought that everything I touched would magically transform for the better. But I was perhaps too blissfully idealistic.

I soon learnt that human beings are the most complex, unpredictable things on earth. They may say one thing, but actually mean another. They are not always honest about their true intentions or motivations. But through the course of my work, I have learnt to ask the right questions long enough to get answers or hints of someone's true intentions. I have learnt that if I were to assume things, my assumptions may just let me down.

A few years ago, while working on retained C-Level executive searches in Japan—alongside colleagues in the US and Europe who were ex-Korn Ferry, ex-Heidrick & Struggles partners—it was drilled into me that the more senior level the search, the more critical it is to ensure that we have every angle covered, therein leaving nothing to chance. For at the C-Level, the available pool of talent is limited; we cannot afford to lose a top executive talent because we failed to get the negotiation right or had read their motivation wrongly.

I have since learnt my "ABC"—Always Be Closing. I have since learnt to ask pre-closing questions at every step of the process, on top of having a small, but healthy dose of paranoia and cynicism. Even when I seemingly have things under control, I would look at devising a Plan B. What happens if it all goes pear-shaped? How would I recover? And what are my contingency plans? When the assignment is headed towards the finishing line, I also need to know the real-no-bullshit-must-have bottom line for both parties in order to close the deal.

The following are some questions that I would ask to seal the deal:

- If we get you the offer you want tomorrow, are you ready to sign the contract?
- Tell me in absolute details what you are looking for to close the deal. I can't promise to get you everything you want, but I need to know at this critical stage.
- Do you foresee any issues with you signing the contract? Have you cleared it with all relevant parties that will have a say in your final decision? What would you do if these parties disagree, even though you are ready to sign?
- What would you do if there is a counter offer?
- Are there areas you are concerned or unsure of that would prevent you from signing the contract? Let's address it now.

Asking the right questions improve my chances of closing the deal. Should the worst-case scenario happens, I am prepared to handle and resolve the issue(s) successfully. And if all things do go well, it is time to pop the champers! In both scenarios, I stand to win!

There is absolutely no room for chance or luck. That is reserved for punters at the racing tracks on weekends. As a practical optimist, I also know that in the sales game, some will become rising rock stars, while others will spiral into mediocrity. Some will even quit and go on their merry way into a different career. Having seen and worked with some very talented people, I am reminded of various critical traits that are consistent in sales winners:

1. **Having a positive personality**
   Working with positive, glass half-full, can-do individuals gives me such a rush. Maintaining a positive mindset and doing things with a zing in your step brings high energy into the environment around you. On the other hand, working with difficult, negative, toxic, passive-aggressive (defiant through inactivity), and sulky individuals is simply draining.

   Someone I used to work with called the two groups of individuals "vampires" and "Santa Clauses". The "vampire" simply drains the life out of you with his or her sinking, stinky attitude, while the "Santa Claus" brings in good cheer and hope to all. Now, this is a good analogy to help you better appreciate the "Santa Clauses" in life. So please leave your vampire fangs at home and come to the office all ready to go go go!

2. **Being humble and teachable**
   Having accumulated an extensive experience in the headhunting industry, I feel like I know enough to tell my trained new hires never to second-guess my judgment over every little thing. That, in my opinion, will only slow down their development and progress. I tell them that there is no need for them to impress me—there will come a time for that. Instead, the fastest way to get up to speed is to listen and apply, listen and apply, and still listen and apply. Never say that something cannot be done until you try. Once you have results to show for, you can then come up with better ideas. Then, I will happily humble myself and the tables can turn.

3. **Having a sense of urgency**
   I am a big fan of the saying "You snooze, you lose." You see, sales is all about speed. Hours, even minutes, count when securing a hot prospect before a competitor gets to him or her first. Sometimes, emailing can be the biggest killer of deals, because we often spend too much time crafting the perfect email that nobody bothers to read anyway, instead of just picking up the phone to call and have a quick, productive conversation. So instead of typing a labouriously long email, I often have to remind myself and others to just pick up the phone and call!

   Do not be known as an artillery gunner: "Gunna do this, gunna do that." Just get it done. What could be worse than not getting something urgent completed as quickly as possible? Why wind up blaming those around you or circumstances, because the blame game only reflects poorly on you.

4. **Quick to take action**
   You are paid a fair wage for your work. In fact, sales can be extremely rewarding when you have results. In sales, actions equal results. There are key activities in a sales job that need to be done to produce results, do these a lot and often enough! Essentially, there are no short cuts to success. Of course, between quality and quantity, you should aim to strike a good balance to ensure that one is never compromised because of the other. Too often, I see people focusing on quantity over quality, which is fine. But once you have the critical mass rolling down the hill, tweak on improving quality. In the wise words of my favourite young billionaire Mark Zuckerberg, founder of Facebook, "Done is better than perfect." So let us get things done!

#44 Is hard work important? What about work-life balance?

"They sure don't make us like they used to." This is a phrase that I have been hearing a lot of lately.

Recently, I have had deep and meaningful discussions with several managers who span various industries in Singapore, Hong Kong, and Japan. When we shared about improving and driving business performances, I sensed a lot of frustration, almost exasperation from these managers, as they try to get their people to focus and execute key activities. It appears that the push for their people to deliver their 100%, plus an additional 10% to rise above mere mediocrity, has been met with much challenges.

This prompted me to reflect on how things were carried out some 15 years ago when I was still a rookie. Were people more hardworking then? Has there been a change in mindset and thinking among the young people today?

These days, you hardly hear someone say: "Man! You must be the hardest working guy in the industry!" It is almost as if hard work is scorned upon. To many, a hardworking lad is simply selling himself short for the company. But to me, this is really a huge compliment. You see, I equate hard work to success. In my opinion, success is not a by-product of smooth charm and dumb luck. Sure, luck does sometimes play a part, but you cannot be lucky all the time. In fact, I also believe that "The harder you work, the luckier you get."

When I first started my career in headhunting in Sydney, I was working for the largest headhunting firm in town. I was one of two Asian consultants in a company of 200 staff. We had a stunningly gorgeous Asian lady with perfect diction working in the banking team, often found having lunches and cocktails with her banking clients and winning tons of business. And then there was me, the Asian guy with a stutter (oh great!), trying to sell talent to the beer-swilling, tough-as-nails construction and engineering industries that were just coming out from a recession and cash-strapped.

Pitched against outstanding colleagues, I took a cold, hard look at my SWOT (Strengths, Weaknesses, Opportunities, Threats) Analysis and recalled telling myself that my only advantage is my good work ethic. I told myself that I would simply have to outwork everyone else to make it to the top biller's list. It took about a year of blood, sweat, and tears before I got where I needed to be. At one of the end-of-quarter award functions, the Managing Director got up and announced: "The highest biller (consultant) of the quarter award goes to a bloke that got there through sheer hard work and resilience—got up time and time again when things didn't seem to go his way…" As you expect, I was pretty chuffed that day.

These days, there is so much hype about striking a work-life balance, and I admittedly would like that balance too. But is work-life balance feasible when you just started out in a new career, or in a career that you do not seem to be getting any traction? Probably not.

Recently, I was training a new generation of rookies when I told them: "If you want to be on top of your game and achieve something meaningful in anything that you do, at times, your life will be unbalanced. There are no shortcuts to the path of glory. You can take three months or a year to learn a new craft—the harder you work on it, the shorter the time to get up to speed. So if you have decided on a new career or direction, why tip toe through the tulips? Why not give it your all, focus 100%, and work your butt off to get to the top of that hill. Then, only when you are assured of the momentum carrying you down hill, take time to pursue the other things in your life."

After all, Steve Jobs and Mark Zuckerberg probably did not have work-life balance when they first started up Apple and Facebook.

#45 Do you have any tips on decision-making?

We make decisions everyday. Some of us are seemingly wired to make laser-sharp decisions, but on the other end of the spectrum, others find it stressful to make even the simplest of decisions, such as what to wear or what to have for lunch.

Years ago, I read in a self-help management book that to be decisive, you need to work on your decision-making muscles. In my own words, this means that the more decisions you make, the more confident you are of your decision-making ability and trusting your instincts to make correct decisions.

At work, people rely on me to make decisions everyday. It is what I am paid to do. These decisions will result in win-win, win-lose, lose-win, or lose-lose outcomes. Some decisions can be made without batting an eye, and others are more complicated, requiring some strategising and deliberating. Some are associated with high risk, but on the flipside higher potential returns. And some are just tough calls to make. But whatever the decision to be made, I do not shrink away from making them.

In good times, I have made decisions to acquire businesses, open new offices in new markets, hire people, invest a substantial amount of money in infrastructure, and promote people. And in bad economic times, I made unpleasant decisions to shut down offices, made some of my staff and colleagues (whom I have worked with for years) redundant, fired non-performers, and cut employees' salary to keep the business afloat.

Of course, not all my decisions achieved stellar outcomes (I wish I had that foresight). In life, you really do not know how things will pan out, but a decision needs to be made nonetheless. So the secret to success is to make more good decisions than bad decisions. This will ensure that you get ahead!

The following are some tips to help you make better decisions:

1. **Simplify things and keep a clear mind**
   There can be a lot to consider when making a decision, but I always try to break it down to the core essentials of why we are making the decision—the other stuff is just background noise to cloud the main issue(s). Being a visual person, I sometimes put down on paper the decision to be made and how the options roll out. Before making a difficult and often complicated decision, I tend to sleep on it before arriving at a decision the next day. I believe some thinking time is wise. For more critical decisions, I usually go for a walk and allow myself time to think though the various outcomes. By the end of my walk, my mind is usually crystal clear on things, or at least have somewhat of a plan mapped out, thanks to some fresh air and exercise. To date, my longest "decision-making walk" lasted two and a half hours.

2. **Be honest, respectful, and fair**
   It is truly tough being a business leader at times. While you have company sales and profit goals to achieve, you also have employees who for different reasons are not performing up to expectation. So naturally, you have to make tough decisions. Since you cannot please everybody all the time, you always make the "right" decision for your people. Here, making the "right" decision does not mean making a "soft" decision. The "right" decision requires you to be honest, respectful, and fair. By being honest, respectful, and fair in all that I do, I can always sleep well at night, no matter how grave a decision I make. Some of the staff whom I have had to make redundant or dismiss over the years, are still good friends whom I catch up with socially. Of course, some would not hesitate to run me over if they see me cross the road, but at least my conscience is clear.

3. **Stand by your decisions but also have a contingency plan**
   Once the decision is made, stand firm in your decision. You have to be fully committed to it. Having said that, the seemingly best decisions can sometimes be blindsided by new developments. With this knowledge, I like to think through various scenarios and devise a Plan B in my back pocket. If you do have to change your decision, do so ever so reluctantly and with good reason.

4. **Done better than perfect**
   Mark Zuckerberg wrote a note to potential investors addressing Facebook's then impending initial public offering. In his note, he mentioned the Hacker's Way. One bit that stood out for me was his belief in the personal ethos that "Done is better than perfect." This, to me, implies the sense of urgency to get things done. Make the decision, set the momentum going, and then tweak it along the way to perfect it. Do not suffer paralysis by analysis and delay making critical decisions. That said, I often postpone making the non-critical, minor decisions, because I have learned that some problems tend to sort themselves out!

#46 How can being an optimist serve my career?

Do you see a glass half-full?

Well, I am a self-professed optimist. Those who know me would probably say that I am a positive person who sees a glass half-full, always taking the optimistic view on the bleakest situation. And yes, I do appear to possess the confidence to be the fixer of a given problem even when the odds are stacked against it. But do you know that being an optimist can be a choice you make?

Now let me ask you this question, "How do you view your life now?"

Surely, a lot must be happening in your life, entailing your family, health, relationships, work, and personal finances, just to name a few. Perhaps some of these facets lend a more positive outlook to your life, while others are less promising. But which view do you choose to take in life?

Most people do not know that I used to stutter as a child and most part of my adulthood. Up to the point when I started my career as an engineer at the Sydney Water Board, I was still stuttering. Then, I dreaded when people asked me where I worked. My answer would sound like an old diesel engine kick-starting on a cold winter's day, "I w... ww… wwww... work for the w... wwww Water Board!"

One day, I decided that I had enough of stuttering for the past twenty over years, and wanted a new start. With that decision, I embarked on curing myself. To "cure" myself of my constant stutters, I read a mountain of self-help and positive-thinking books over a period of several years.

Those positive-thinking books gave me the confidence boost and motivated me to fix my stuttering. Once I decided to put a stop to my stuttering, I worked on improving my pronunciation. I found words that I was comfortable articulating to replace words that begin with "w" or "c", which I could not quite grasp. Just like that, the problem was mostly solved! I felt liberated when I discovered how I could get my way around those difficult-to-pronounce words. My confidence grew and I became more willing to hold a conversation. I even took on public speaking! That changed the course of my career as I got the assurance to quit my job as an engineer and eventually became a headhunter. With this career change, I was talking non-stop to people everyday, or at least from 9am to 6pm.

After overcoming my speech impediment, the new optimism and can-do mentality placed me in good stead in my new career. But over the years, I realised that blind positive-thinking alone is not enough to bring about results. That is when I cultivated the practical part to sealing success.

A principle I learned about being a practical optimist is to ignore the noise around you and focus on what you can control. Maintain laser-like focus on the key fundamentals of success—working smart and working really hard.

Surely, there is bound to be negative news in the media simply because bad news sells! It is oftentimes easy to be paralysed by the negativity. You start to blame the distractions—the circumstances, incompetent people, the economy, the government (or other governments for that matter). But instead of focusing on these negativities, you are better off focusing on actions and activities that will lead to accomplishments and results.

I remember learning a lesson or two about being positive when I read the biography of General Colin Powell. He was the Commander of the US Armed Forces and Chairman of the Joint Chiefs of Staff during the George W. Bush era. He directly oversaw 28 major crisis including Operation Desert Storm. An extremely capable career military man, General Colin Powell was nicknamed the "reluctant warrior", because President Bush (both senior and junior) would make the gung-ho decisions to invade Saudi Arabia and Iraq, but General Powell would be the practical voice of reason to play out the longer term implications of going to war—the overall cost incurred by America, the occupation, the transition, the handover, and the exit strategy. Through his story, General Colin Powell taught me the principle of visualising not only success, but also the possibilities along the way.

These days, I face new challenges all the time—some big, some small. By practising practical optimism, I have greater confidence in tackling them to the best of my ability and delivering a positive impact.

#47 How do I stay motivated and driven?

Commitment, motivation, and drive are some underlying attributes that serve individuals and teams. A successful entrepreneur once told me: "Growing a business and managing people can be easy if you hire smart, self-driven, and self-motivated people." Seems simple enough, but is it really so?

You see, hiring smart, or smart enough people (we cannot all be rocket scientists or the guys in the sitcom *The Big Bang Theory*) is more straightforward when we can access their mark of intelligence. But how can we track their motivational level too? Can we really use Maslow's Hierarchy of Needs as the basis for analysis to motivate a staff to do what is required to perform above expectation? Is the promise to satisfy one's higher needs truly enough?

In this world, all of us are wired differently. Not all of us are highly disciplined, and possess a clear and focused mind. Not all of us are self-driven and spurred by an inner source of motivation.

For many, money is a key motivation. Their lives revolve around growing their wealth—and more is never enough—as well as all the things that one can buy with it—branded items, an enviable lifestyle, financial security and freedom.

Climbing up the corporate ladder, and with it the power, respect, and the prestige of having an important title and responsibility is also a very appealing proposition for a lot of people in life. In a bid to enjoy a better status and position, they have no qualms about working towards their next success. These individuals can be naturally competitive, possessing the need to win and emerge as the alpha male in the pack.

While some are motivated by their innate want to become more in life, others are motivated through outward factors. For instance, the director of a recruitment company I once worked in tried to flame employees' drive by encouraging us to get in debt.

"Yeah, go buy that apartment and that new BMW series looks good!"

To rouse our appetite for more, he would offer his brand new Porsche as a weekend prize for the top performer of the quarter. The idea is, if an individual is in a comfort zone and not goal-driven, he or she will just auto-cruise. Work would be simply going through the motions day after day and the results mediocre. So, by getting in debt with the purchase of say, a new car, he or she will find reason to get out of bed with a zing!

Sometimes, implanting a dream, much like in the movie *Inception*, works. Some of us need external motivations, such as group goals, to move forward in life. These team players need to feel that others around them are striving alongside one another towards a higher mission.

Essentially, the trick to motivating someone is to know who needs what and when. When the motivation is gone, it can be likened to having the lights switched on, but with no one at home. This is when you need to look for something else to reignite that fire.

#48 How do I maintain a high energy level?

Over the years, one of the things I have learnt about myself is the need to manage my energy level. This is especially important when I am required to be alert, sharp, articulate and on top of my game most of the time. If world-class athletes and football players have special diets and downtime to keep them at their peak performance during game time, I figured I need to do the same to achieve a similar effect on myself.

I know it is probably different for everyone, but I am a morning person. No, I am not one of those early morning folks who get up at the crack of dawn to go for a 10-kilometre run, but from the instant I pry my eyes open, I spring out of bed, raring to go. I usually keep my breakfast light and then I am off to the "factory".

I found 9am to 11am to be my most productive time of the day. This is the window period when I attend to urgent, complicated, or sensitive agenda items.

At 11am, I treat myself to a good cup of coffee. This gives me the chance to get out of the office, take in some fresh air, and stretch the legs. Following that short break, work continues until lunch time.

For me, lunch comprises of a salad with chicken or tuna—basically lots of vegetables and protein and as little carbohydrate as possible. If I have a heavy meal of rice, bread, noodles or pasta during lunch, I will be a zombie nodding off by 3pm.

Not everyone is productive in the mornings. Many have trouble getting up in the mornings. Throughout the day, they appear constantly tired, lacking vitality and energy. And there could be tons of reasons—mental exhaustion, stress, as well as poor nutrition and sleep habits.

When your lifestyle choices begin to affect your performance at work, it is probably time to address them. But having said that, weekends should come with a totally different set of rules. This is a time to re-charge the old batteries. Indulge in the occasional good food and take cat naps. There is after all a time to play, as well as a time to work.

#49 What are some time management tips?

AT

The advancement of technology should have made us more efficient and effective. Right now, we have in our hands tools that can look up an address, fix an appointment, book a flight, on top of hundreds of other functions.

Unfortunately, technology is panning out to be like a lot of dynamite; it could help you blast your way to the next gold mine, but it could also kill a lot of people if not handled well.

With the increased demands that many companies are expecting from their employees, it is becoming even more important to work smarter and faster. But working hard and smart can be obstructed when you allow yourself to be absorbed in activities that suck your time away, much like a vampire that drains your blood.

Avoid some of the worst productivity killers in the workplace and you will find better use of your time. The following are pointers to note for better time management:

1. **Refrain from engaging social media at work**
   Social media has been likened to drugs or cigarettes, the kind that you constantly have to take to get your fix. And just like drugs or cigarettes, they do not really serve any functional purpose. And the wider your social network, the more fixes you require.

   Unless your job title says Social Media Executive, Facebooking and twittering should be left to after work hours or lunch time. Each message you post takes away precious minutes that you are better off attending to pressing work. Imagine how you would feel if someone in your team is constantly on Facebook when the team project is already behind schedule—exactly how your manager feels when he sees your Twitter page every time he walks past your cubicle!

2. **Do not type the same information over and over**
   Have you heard of something called templates? Well, if you have not, it is high time you learn about it. If you have standard "boilerplate" information that is frequently used, create a template that you can quickly tap into and copy to customise it per recipient.

3. **Good organisation of information**
   Even though you are not an administrator, there is no excuse not to be specific and proper when it comes to organising your files. And organise your files in a way that makes sense to you and those who might be using them. That way, you would not need to spend half an hour trying to locate that one contract. Or worse, spending half a day recreating the entire document from scratch because you cannot find it.

4. **Communicate right the first time**
   When your email requires more than two rounds of editing, you should really just pick up the phone to convey the message. One of the biggest time suckers is when bad communication causes misunderstandings, and more time is wasted trying to undo the misunderstanding. Instead of attending to actual matters, time is now spent writing long-winded emails, when in fact a short conversation can clear matters up readily. So if you have a complicated or sensitive topic at hand, the best rule of thumb is to call the person first, then follow up with a recap email. You could save hours and avoid all the hassle!

5. **Keep focused in cyber space**
   The Internet has so much distractions. Every time you head out for one purpose, you unwittingly end up addressing another. Before you know it, an hour is gone and nothing work-related has been achieved. If you suffer from attention deficit of some sort, create a "grocery list" to keep you focused. This will train you to go online, do what

you need, and then exit without sidetracking. To counter such activities, some companies even install a tracker on their network to monitor the amount of employees' productive hours based on the Internet traffic they amass. So beware!

6. **Hold fruitful meetings**
   Many people hate meetings, but these meetings are a necessary workplace evil. If you really look at it, it is not the meetings per se, it is the time wasted digressing agendas among an unprepared lot, and a general lack of time control. So while you want to grant participants enough time to be engaged, it is up to you to keep track of the topics and be bold enough to intervene when a meeting deviates from its objective. Surely, not everyone is a great meeting leader. So if someone else is chairing the meeting and the discussion is heading the wrong direction, offer to step in and help facilitate if possible.

7. **Minimise office chats**
   It is important to facilitate good working relationships, and office chats do build rapport among colleagues. But if you find your work constantly disrupted every fifteen minutes with the random "visitor", you really need to reassert yourself and the importance of your time. Set up a schedule so you know when you should gently postpone office chats and when you could indulge in them.

8. **Avoid cleaning up the mess of others**
   If you find yourself dealing with this chronic problem, it is time to take action. Time spent on other people's issues is limiting what you can spend on yours—the ones that you are ultimately accountable for. So you need to determine the best course of action on ways to deal with this. If the person is a subordinate, then this is the perfect mentoring/coaching opportunity on performance improvement. If he or she is your equivalent, have a frank, tactful sit-down to discuss how this colleague could succeed on his or her own terms. The key is not to make it confrontational. Instead, focus on solving his or her root problem at work so that you are no longer needed to attend to their inadequacies.

9. **Refrain from piling up work that your superior should be doing**
   In my previous workplace, I had a colleague who would never say "no" to her manager. Her workload kept piling, but her proficiency in complicated computer systems was limiting her output. So she ended up working overtime every day. She eventually became a go-to person whenever our manager wished to keep her hands clean. My colleague was thus overlooked for a number of promotions so she could continue to do the "dirty" work. If this sounds like you, it is time to have a conversation with a human resource personnel to work this through. As in every office, there will be times when vampires are lurking around, but with the right tactics that work as the proverbial garlic to ward them off, you will necessarily see a spike in your productivity!

#50 What must I do in my first 100 days at work?

So you went through three rounds of gruesome interviews and have finally gotten the job. Your long-awaited new beginning has come, but what should you do now? How would your new colleagues take towards you? What type of impression should you give them? What is the working style of your new superior?

I believe these are questions that would go through your mind as you plan to settle in and maybe even get into your superior's good book. Well, 100 days seems an eternity when you know everyone in your company is watching your every move. But it also seems rather short when you are required to pick things up quickly. So it is indeed not easy being the new kid on the block.

As in other developed countries, the employment climate in Singapore is highly competitive and a lot can be expected of employees. The first 100 days at your new job is thus an important time as you reposition yourself career-wise. The following is some advice as you kickstart this new job:

1. **Listen and learn**
   This is definitely sound advice. God gave us two ears and a mouth so that we listen more than we speak. He also placed each ear on different sides of our head so that we can listen from all directions, as well as both sides of the story. If you have just gotten yourself a managerial role, your staff will either be very distant towards you initially, or they will warm up to you, immediately filling you in with the happenings in the company. Now, there is nothing wrong with either, but a line

must be drawn. You must learn to do a background check and take in information objectively. You must also learn as much as possible from your direct superior. Identify the gap that was left by your predecessor. Work very closely with your superior, understand his plans for the future, as well as what he wants to execute first. But do not just be a soldier who obeys every command. Feel free to contribute and make healthy challenges if need be. Take initiatives to highlight yourself. There is a reason why you have been selected for this job.

2. **Manage your expectations**

Managing your expectations is highly critical during this period. There may be lots of backlogs waiting to be dumped on you, especially when replacing a role that has been vacant for many months. By this time, the covering staff would have had enough of spillover duties from the resignee. But be careful. Do not allow yourself to become overwhelmed by allowing things to be dumped on your lap. It is understandable for you to want to come across as a friendly and supportive teammate at the beginning, but you cannot possibly say "yes" to everyone in the team.

If you start becoming the "yes" man, you may lose focus of core duties that you are paid to engage. Always check with your superior and align his or her priorities to yours before embarking on any task. Be accountable for your top duties and update your superior when a task at hand has been completed. Approach your colleagues if you require more information or face challenges halfway. Do not sit around and wait for a miracle to happen—they are not fortune-tellers who can read you. You must also be very mindful of the channel through which you report your activities. Do not override authority or get instructions from people you are not supposed to. This is the time when you are still entitled to under promise and over deliver. So for now, take it slow, digest, analyse, and then accelerate.

3. **Leave a good impression**

First impression counts. The first 100 days of work is the period when colleagues form an initial impression of you. This is the period when you are judged. So be punctual and prompt for all things related to work—this includes arriving on time for meetings and even company drinking sessions. Feel free to demonstrate that you are willing to go the extra mile for your team and the company. Whether you emerge as a new team player in the company depends very much on your level of enthusiasm; you could be identified as an energy generator or an energy zapper. So be the one to bring up the spirit of your team by celebrating the successes of your teammates, be they big or small. Book your colleagues for lunches and be genuinely interested in their lives. Sure you do not expect yourself to be everyone's best buddy, but at least create opportunities for others to know you better. I am pretty sure people will begin to place their faith and trust in your authority, capability, and most importantly, your integrity.

Whether your first 100 days is going to be a living hell or an open heaven on earth, depends really on your doing! In the words of Donald Trump, "What separates the winners from the losers is how a person reacts to each new twist of fate."

#51 How do I win an argument?

To succeed in business, you have to be able to win arguments convincingly. Of course, you cannot expect to win all the time. Win some, lose some (hopefully there are more wins than losses).

To increase your chance of winning, preparation is important. You cannot just go into a business argument and wing it. You need to have all the facts at your fingertips to back up your argument. The better prepared you are, the more confident you will be in your delivery. Since people tend to remember opening and closing comments, be sure to keep them concise and impactful.

Next, know your opponents. Know what they want to get out of the argument, and what they are willing to settle for. With this understanding, you can better craft your responses to give them what they will settle for, yet get what you want out of it.

Think win-win. No one likes to lose especially in a room full of people. Do not overtly bruise their ego. Save them some dignity, and allow them a graceful exit. Leave something on the table for them to walk away with, without them feeling that they have lost completely.

Be quick-witted and come up with compromises. Think outside of the box when offering alternate solutions. Do not repeat yourself though—it is plain boring! The art of persuasion is key. Win hearts and minds through a combination of emotional hooks and logical, well thought out arguments.

No one likes to feel that they have to swallow what is pushed down their throats. So look at selling not just the features, but also the benefits when getting others to accept your ideas. Think of how your idea can also leave a positive impact on them.

Make eye contact with everyone in an argument. Do not forget a smile here and a nod there. It is harder for people to disagree when they are smiling and nodding along with you. Communicate your thoughts clearly and simply. If appropriate, liven up the mood by using humour—this works really well for me.

When you are speaking, do not let someone cut you off mid-sentence. If that happens, do not hesitate to say "Excuse me, can I finish what I have to say?" That person will most likely not interrupt your speech during the presentation again.

Stay calm, relaxed, and watch your body language. Do not cross your arms or get emotionally charged. Composure is good in situations like these.

At the end of the day, it does not matter who wins. If the argument reaches an impasse, it is sometimes better to agree to disagree and walk away with your pride intact.

#52 How should I ask for a raise?

There are two key things to remember when you contemplate asking for that next raise—if you do not ask you would never get it, and what you want might not be what you are getting.

Asking for a raise seems to be a knotty issue. So when really is the best time to be asking for a raise?

In my opinion, the best time to be asking for that raise is during the annual performance review. This is a time when you review your wins, successes, and overachievements. If you have had a good year and an outstanding performance to show for, your superior will almost be expecting you to ask for a raise. If that is so, then name a number or a percentage increase.

But how much should you be asking for if you have had a good performing year? Well, the raise should at least cover the rise of inflation, say at 3% to 4%. However, you should be aiming for 10% to 20% if the company truly values you.

It is common to negotiate a little, but keep it cordial—you really can be spared the awkwardness from a post-salary discussion the next day. Do state clearly your intention and allow your superior to think it over. But never ask for a raise via an email. It is better to ask for a raise in person, when you look straight into your superior's eyes—it is harder for him or her to reject your request this way.

There are also better suited days to ask for the much coveted raise. Not on a Monday for sure. This is often the busiest day of the week. Besides, your superior is still adjusting to the work week after a restful weekend. Not on a Friday either. If your superior have had a bad week, your request could be the perfect outlet to dump all of his or her frustrations on you. So Tuesdays, Wednesdays, and Thursdays are your best bets.

If for some reason(s), your superior is unable to offer a raise in cash terms, then ask for additional perks. This could be in the form of entertainment allowance, mobile phone allowance, parking allowance, transport allowance, a gym membership, training opportunities, or sponsoring your higher education.

But never ever play poker by saying that you have a better offer outside. He might just call your bluff!

Finally, never ask for a salary raise if you have had a bad performing year. Count yourself lucky that you are still employed and on a payroll!

#53 How do I survive a business lunch?

Most of us have never attended etiquette lessons. Me neither! So, what are the dos and don'ts when attending a business lunch, and how do you make a positive impact in such an appointment?

The following are some tips that I have gathered along the way:

- Be punctual. This seems obvious, but it is in reality, not a well-practised habit.
- Save the best seat for your guest—usually the seat with a view. While not doing so is not a showstopper, it is certainly a classy detail to note.
- Switch your phone to silent mode. Refrain from looking at your phone for messages and emails during the business lunch.
- If you are lunching with your superior, and supposing he or she would be footing the bill, choose a dish that is cheaper than his or her order. You do not want to come across as an opportunist freeloader.
- Avoid ordering difficult to eat food. Food that requires you to get your hands dirty such as prawns, crabs, and lobsters are out unless they are de-shelled. Other food that can be messy to eat include spare ribs and chicken wings.
- In Asia, most of us do not drink alcohol at lunch. But if your guest is having one, go ahead and order a glass of wine or champagne. You can sip a little, but never to the point of being tipsy before heading back to the office. Drinks to definitely avoid include red bull vodka and long island tea. These are drinks better left for the Friday night party.

There is also an art to dining, if I could call it that. Firstly, the napkins go on your lap. If you have to leave the table to visit the washroom, leave your napkin on your chair, not on the table.

Be engaging during the conversation. Do not get distracted by other activities in the restaurant. When it comes to the use of cutlery, my rule of thumb is always start with the cutlery on the outside and work my way towards the plate. Other than that, the usual dining etiquette applies—do not talk with your mouth full. And obviously, sip your soup, not slurp!

Then comes the time to pay after the meal. Personally, I cannot bear the awkwardness when everyone fights over the bill at the end of the meal. If you intend to pay for the meal, do it discreetly. Leave your credit card with the waiter before your guest arrives, so that the bill will be directed to you when the meal is done.

Finally, I fancy bringing my guests to a familiar restaurant—a place where I patronise frequently and the waiters know me. This way, I am almost guaranteed a good service. This restaurant would be like the diners in the sitcom *Cheers*, where everyone knows your name. That way, my clients will be impressed with the level of attention and service we get during our meal.

#54 What should I consider when I have to relocate overseas?

The world is increasingly a smaller place. If you are seeking an opportunity to live and work overseas, there is never an easier time for you to do so anywhere in the world, if you possess the skills and experience which employers seek.

In my opinion, two of the most stressful events in life are changing jobs and moving to a new place. And when you relocate overseas—you are effectively juggling both at one go. And that is one mega-combo!

Having moved my career and family from Sydney to Singapore, Singapore to Tokyo, and then back to Singapore again, I picked up first-hand a few useful tips on relocating and settling into a new environment that might be useful for you.

Do not underestimate the cost of relocating overseas

Here are some things to look into as you pack up in your home country and get ready to move:

- Getting out of your current lease if you are renting.
- Selling big-ticket items such as your car, white goods, and furniture even if it is usually at a loss.
- Cancelling your mobile phone plan and paying a penalty for prematurely ending the contract.
- A hotel stay for a few days to a week when you are without a home and waiting for the big trip.
- Transporting all your belongings via sea or air to the new abode.

Once you arrive at the new country, there are other costs involved as you begin to settle in. Firstly, there is the deposit for a new rental apartment. This can range from two to six months rent upfront, on top of the fee payable to a real estate agent for his service, which is usually equivalent to a month's rent.

Other costs involve international school fees if there are kids involved, buying a new set of wheels, white goods, furniture, and household items. You will also need to sign up for new mobile phone plans and the list goes on…

A lot of these little things, plus some big-ticket items really do add up! With this in consideration, employers tend to provide relocation allowances to offset some of these costs. However, I notice fewer "expat" packages being offered. In replacement are the less attractive "local", or "semi-local" packages. So instead of digging into your own pockets for costs that should otherwise be defrayed, negotiate and agree on all your terms upfront, to avoid the shock of burning a hole in your bank account before you even embark on your dream job overseas.

Despite all that costs incurred, one of the more attractive things about relocating, in some instances, is moving from a high income tax rate country such as Australia, Canada, and UK, to a country like Singapore and Hong Kong, where the income tax rate is comparatively "friendly". And this makes such a move really worth considering.

Have fun with a new language

If you are considering a move to somewhere within Asia, notwithstanding Singapore and Hong Kong, language could be a real barrier. Unless you are an adept linguist, it is not easy to attain fluency in a new language quickly, even with lessons. So be prepared to use the most basic forms of communication to get your message across—be it using body language, or even drawing. So it comes as no surprise when expats walk into restaurants having to "flap their wings" to order a plate of chicken, or make "moo" noises to order a beef dish.

Into the first month when I relocated to Tokyo, I kept a handwritten sheet of paper with instructions for the local taxi driver to send me back to my apartment. I would pray to God that the taxi driver does not turn back with questions, for I could have done nothing but stare back at him. I would have had no idea how to get myself home if I had lost that piece of paper!

In the beginning, I even had to invite my secretary to my apartment to show me how to operate the air-con, television, and washing machine. Since all the controls were labelled in Japanese, she offered to help print the labels in English and stuck it on the controls. Something as simple as operating a household appliance has become something that we take for granted, until we begin to live in a foreign country where language becomes a barrier.

So with the help of Japanese friends and colleagues, it took me three long months before I settled into a comfortable routine in Tokyo. And with that sense of normalcy, life was sweet again!

Even though my relocations had been costly and needed some adjusting to, I would do it all over again in a heartbeat, because these experiences have enriched my life. I would also like to think that I have become a more interesting person as a result.

#55 How do I protect myself in a recession?

During a recession, companies cut headcounts and budgets. Rarely does one get past a day without hearing a retrenchment of some sort.

For those of you who were once laid off, you probably never saw it coming. But did you at least learn something from the last retrenchment? Would you be better prepared should recessionary times befall again?

The following are some pointers to help you prepare for tough times, so that you can better weather the storm should it blow:

1. **Make yourself indispensable**
   A downturn is the best opportunity for the management to clean the house. Just because your manager never told you off for consistently coming in late, going for long lunches, or Facebooking the entire day at work does not mean that he is unaware of your actions. Chances are he or she did the same at your age. Instead, make yourself indispensible to the company. Make your contributions count.

2. **Avoid recession-sensitive industries**
   If you had known that Lehman Brothers was going to close its doors six months before it happened, would you still apply for a job with them? History, if it has taught us anything at all, has taught us that the banking industry has always been one of the most economy-sensitive industries. So when the financial climate looks grey, you may want to consider sectors that are more stable.

3. **Look at recession-friendly careers**
   Life still goes on during recessionary times, and there will still be jobs that thrive, maybe even more so during a downturn. Some of such trades would be linked to:

   - **Education**
     There will always be jobs for teachers. Kids will still go to school and many unemployed adults would choose to learn new skills.

   - **Military or any uniformed group**
     This option gives you six to ten years of guaranteed employment, unless you decide to do something crazy.

   - **Gambling**
     When times are bad and people face retrenchment, there is a seemingly attractive way to make money without having to hold a job.

   - **Debt management companies**
     Financial crisis is more prevalent during bad times. And many who are cash strapped need guidance to help tide them through.

More importantly, never stop networking and remember to never burn bridges at work. One more friend equals one less enemy—you never know when you might need to call in a favour at work.

PART SEVEN

GETTING PROMOTED!

"The best job goes to the person who can get it done without passing the buck or coming back with excuses."

–Charles Schwab

#56 Do I want to be a manager or leader?

A question I always pose to potential managers in training is, "Do you want to be a manager?" It would seem at first that this is a rather silly question. After all, it is a natural progression for someone to head up the corporate ladder—move from a front line producer role to a management role that heads a business unit. However, management is a huge responsibility and not many succeed in doing it well. This explains why tons of management books are written.

In the headhunting industry, we are a pure play professional services business, without major capital investments tied up in manufacturing plants or warehouses, with no supply chain, or logistics issues to worry about. Our business is not a complex one. Sure, the right business strategies and company structure are important to succeed in this industry, but the most important element is really our people.

Motivating our people to perform at their best and collectively deliver stellar performances is ultimately the yardstick every manager is measured against. In order to do so consistently, the retention of key people is vital. In today's market, employees with skills and talents are highly sought after and hence the freedom to choose whether to follow you or move to another better option.

Not all people in management positions can lead. I am sure we all have encountered bad leaders in our careers. Experts believe that through evolution, for survival, animals and humans are all programmed to instinctively evaluate leadership potential of who we want to follow. Research has also clearly shown that the team with a good leader always outperforms. So what are attributes that make a good leader whom others will follow? The following are my picks:

1. **Trustworthiness**
   Trust is the basis of all relationships. People want a leader who would keep to his or her word, back them up in times of crisis, and take the lead in good or bad times. Initially, people might give you the benefit of the doubt. But take heed that trust is something that must be earned in the long run through your actions, not just mere words.

2. **Decisiveness**
   There are no certainties in life, which makes it all the more important for a good leader to have the foresight and wisdom to make educated, informed guesses, and then bite the bullet and make decisions. Of course, not all decisions are going to turn out right. In the event something goes pear-shaped, a good leader reassesses the situation, and finds new ways to fix it or steer the course. The ability to give clear directions is what people expect of a leader.

3. **Being a player/manager**
   It is my opinion that people today do not blindly follow the leader's instructions. Perhaps this is the Gen Y Syndrome. Now more than ever, leaders must be prepared to roll up their sleeves and show the younger generation how things are done, and then most importantly, delegate, delegate, and delegate. And this to me is the key role of a manager—to delegate so more can be achieved collectively. Since no one likes to be told what to do, it becomes more effective when they feel that the leader is doing it with them.

Having said that, I do tell my subordinates: "Don't tell me it can't be done, until you have tried it." If I can show them that something can be done, there is no reason why they cannot. To be a convincing role model, a leader needs to know what he or she is doing. This leader must be competent. I have seen too many cases where leaders are hired from another industry to lead headhunting firms—their leadership skills are not being questioned until a crisis hit during an economic downturn, and suddenly, the lack of competence or familiarity with the basics of the business becomes evident.

4. **Be visionary**
A good leader must have the ability to clearly envisage where the individual and the business are positioned three to five years from now, and have a plan to get there. In professional businesses, where its staff is adequately paid to meet more than their basic lifestyle needs, the most important staff retention strategy is to have a career plan for them. As such, interest in your subordinates' short and long-term career objectives makes for a desirable trait in a leader.

5. **Connecting with others**
A good leader must be able to connect and communicate the team's vision, strategy, and decisions, clearly and frequently. Emotional attachment is like a roller coaster. We may have our good and bad days, but the constant reminder of the bigger picture is important—to achieve something spectacular and the buy-in to that mission is key to keep everyone engaged.

So back to my earlier question, "Do you want to be a manager?" Before you put your hand up, ask yourself why do you want to be a manager? Is being a manager about boosting your ego, ambition, finances, status, power, or a combination of all these things? Whatever the reason, you must want to be a manager, and a successful one at that, because you want to take the lead.

#57 How can I avoid the perils of a young manager?

During one of my career counselling sessions with a group of MBA students, I learned that almost every one of them would like to become a manager straight after graduating. Knowing better that people management skills is something you pick up through years of work experience, and not just an MBA, I told the students that it may not be a realistic expectation, not immediately at least.

As it turned out, most of the students were not very pleased with my comment, and some even appeared clearly agitated. It was not a pretty sight at all!

Looking back, I started managing my first employee when I was 25 years old. I had no management skills to speak of then. I thought back of past superiors, their good and bad traits, and tried to develop qualities that I felt were worthy of emulating. I thought that would be good enough. But as I began managing more staff, I felt that I had exhuasted all role models whom I could make references to.

How was I supposed to manage conflicts between colleagues when I did not experience such disputes in the past? How was I supposed to deal with an employee who sold the company out when I never knew someone who did that in my previous companies? Wait a minute, is there a guidebook for all these?

With or without any guidance, these are some issues that call for appropriate and immediate actions. And as a manager, you just have to do what is right and in the best interest of the company whether you like it or not.

That would mean terminating the subordinate caught applying for other jobs, or Facebooking the entire time and neglecting his or her key performance indicators. It would also mean giving a subordinate a kick in the backside when he or she is habitually late for work.

Being someone who dislikes conflicts, I do not like to carry out punitive measures for an act that is not desired at the work place. But many a time, you need to grit your teeth in order to solve a bigger problem.

This is something I learned the hard way, when I was working in a call centre straight after serving my National Service. Then, I was put in a supervisory trial after more than a year into the job, to manage a team of colleagues for a brief period. At that time, I thought it should be simple leading a group of people who were previously my peers. But I knew otherwise when some of these colleagues started to take extra long breaks in the pantry, logged in to the system late, and some even decided to go home after lunch. Since they were my peers, I felt the need to keep mum about it.

However, such conduct could not be kept from the management forever. It did not take long before I was found covering up for them. As a result, I was suspended from the trial and was returned to my previous role.

If I had the courage to confront my colleagues then, things would have been vastly different. Yes, they would have probably disliked me for telling on them, but as a team lead, I was paid to ensure things went according to plan.

Today, I am still learning as I carry out the role of a manager each day. If you are just like me, carrying the liability of a baby face, here is what you can do:

1. **Maintain a high level of self-awareness**
   Those who exhibit the lack of high self-awareness fail to sometimes recognise their strengths and weaknesses. More often than not, they tend to think more of themselves than they really are, and do not bow

down to mistakes. I was like that when I was in my teens, but I have since learned to reflect on myself more and am where I am today as a result.

2. **Watch your delivery of speech**
   The same set of Powerpoint slides can be delivered in various ways by different people. Likewise, the same content can be communicated in varied ways. At work, we need to maintain a level of professionalism in our exchanges with others. Our subordinates, being emotional beings too, need to be treated with regard too. This means no reprimanding of subordinates in public, and no curt emails. It helps for you to be more conscious in the way you approach others. This way, you will at least be respected for the way you manage yourself and others.

3. **Always think of the big picture**
   I failed in my supervisory trial, as I was afraid to get into the bad books of my colleagues. In doing so, I failed to look at the bigger picture. Instead of focusing on what was more important in professional terms, which was essentially the company's interest and my career development, I was more concerned about what my colleagues thought of me. If I had known any better then, I would have pointed out a wrongdoing, but in the most appropriate manner.

Essentially, the ability to manage is something earned through real experiences. It is not simply a by-product of an MBA or PhD. The role of management can be best carried out when you maintain a consistent value that you uphold regardless of the situation encountered. Challenging these values under various unforeseen situations will play a big part in sharpening your management acumen and preparing you better for the role someday.

#58 How do I run an effective meeting?

SP

Most meetings can be a complete waste of time. If the meeting involves a room full of staff, it can really work out to be a massive waste of the company's resources; just think of everyone's hourly charge for all those unproductive hours spent in the meeting room!

As such, hold meetings only when it is absolutely necessary. And as a rule of thumb, meetings should not need to exceed an hour. A meeting any longer than that is deemed no longer productive as the attention span of staff wanes significantly.

As much as it is a dread to some, there are others who just love meetings. They will call a meeting for everything—even a meeting to plan for the next meeting!

But meetings are not meaningless either. Usually, meetings run more efficiently when there is an agenda with clear topics to cover. And if punctuality tends to be an issue at meetings, I find that starting your meetings at an odd time like 10.15am works in getting people to arrive more promptly.

To ensure the efficiency of meetings, do not hesitate to get them to cut to the chase. You could also help to summarise their arguments to keep their presentation brief.

Most of the time, the best meetings are the ones that are short, but impactful. Say what is needed clearly and to the point, agree on some action points, and have some clear tasks assigned.

#59 How do I fire someone?

S P

A common pitfall among managers is the need to be well-liked by others. Surely, there is nothing to not like about being the nice manager, but if you want a career in management, you must accept that leading others is not you running for a popularity contest. So rule with an iron fist, but slip on a velvet glove—be the steel behind a soft front.

As a manager, firing a staff is something you do from time to time. If this is something that you cannot do, then you should not be managing them in the first place. But before you decide to fire someone, you might want to give him or her the opportunity to turn the situation around. The following is what you can do before sealing that decision to fire someone:

- Discuss performance issues in person.
- Give a verbal warning in front of a witness. This witness can be a human resource manager or a manager from another department.
- If the verbal warning did not bring about the desired change in behaviour or performance, the next step is to issue a written warning. This warning letter serves as the "last chance saloon".

And when it is time to let the person go, only because everything else had failed, keep it aligned to the local labour laws legislated. Inform the staff why and when he or she is going. Be firm and clear. Do not repeat yourself. If it is due to poor performance or conduct, avoid getting emotional over it. Do not feel the need to apologise as you would have already given plenty of warnings.

I usually let people go on a Friday so that the one being fired, as well as others in the office has time over the weekend to recover from a sudden exit. This helps to buffer the awkwardness come the following Monday.

If the firing is a reason through no fault of theirs, such as a company restructuring or downsizing, apologise and try to part on good terms. Offer to help them to find something new if you have the right network to do so.

AFTERWORD

Thank you for reading this book! We hope the wisdom and insights have given you not only a fresh approach in your search for that dream job, but also ways to grow your career once you have found it!

We would love to hear from you and receive your feedback. While it is not possible to cover every question you wish to ask in this book, your comments could inspire new chapters to future editions. Email us at feedback@alchemylearninglab.com

We wish you the best of luck and as the saying goes, "Success is a journey, not a destination!" So giddy-up!